Following A Legend

Strategic Lessons In Transition And Succession

DR. DAVE BURROWS

One Rib Publications
Nassau, The Bahamas
www.oneribpublications.com
oneribpublications@gmail.com

Following a Legend: Strategic Lessons in Transition and Succession
Copyright © 2020 by David Burrows
Published 2024.

Table of Contents

Epigraph

"Transforming followers into leaders and leaders into agents of Change"

Myles Munroe

"In The Kingdom, Ambassadors do not determine their next assignment; the King alone decides"

Dave Burrows

Preface

There are people who come along once in a lifetime to bless and transform the world. Myles Munroe was one of those people. Rising from poverty in Bain Town, Nassau, The Bahamas, as one of eleven children, he possessed God-given gifts and talents that made room for him on the world's largest and most prominent stages and eventually gave him access to heads of state and powerful leaders in the fields of business, entertainment, politics, and society.

His lifelong motto was evident from his youth: "Transforming followers into leaders and leaders into agents of change." Myles Munroe was both a transformer and an agent of change. As a teenager he led a movement called Youth with the Truth which took the gospel to young people throughout The Bahamas. The movement expanded exponentially when he formed a gospel R&B group known as The Visionaires. The group swept The Bahamas, attracting large crowds and with thousands coming to Christ. The popularity of The Visionaires prompted a meeting between the young Munroe and then-prime minister of The Bahamas Sir Lynden Pindling, who marveled at Munroe's influence over the youth. This meeting sparked a friendship and mutual respect rarely seen between individuals their age.

Myles later went to college at Oral Roberts University (ORU) and excelled once again. He was mentored by Oral Roberts himself and became a member of staff while still attending the school. He worked in the Chaplain's Office and Missions Department, and this is where my front-row seat to the legend began. Although we were from the same island and grew up in the same community, our paths never crossed until I arrived at ORU. He grew up as a preacher; I grew up as a gangster. He was born in the ghetto; the ghetto was born in me. Both of us ended up at ORU at the invitation of my sister Marilyn Burrows Gool who was a close friend and compatriot of Myles's. He went to ORU to expand his knowledge and prepare for life and ministry. I went there to get out of trouble and away from the environments that had left me on the doorstep of the consequences of the streets.

He became my mentor at ORU and influenced my transition from sinner to saint, from a gangster on the streets to a leader and agent of change. My life changed and my trajectory changed because of my encounter with Myles Munroe. At his invitation, I became a cofounder of Bahamas Faith Ministries (BFM) along with Richard Pinder and Henry Francis and served as its first youth pastor. I traveled with Myles Munroe often, particularly in the early years as he began traversing the globe. He provided opportunities for me at major platforms, which provided the impetus for me to expand my influence in the world. I served as vice president of both Bahamas Faith Ministries and Myles Munroe International (MMI) for a number of years.

Myles Munroe had a passion for the developing world (at the time known as the Third World), for the oppressed and the marginalized. His message and words were always empowering. He encouraged us who were his friends and contemporaries from the developing world, to change our thinking from consumers to owners, from mission fields to missionaries. He taught that freedom carries a burden, a responsibility of the oppressed to ensure that the cycle of subjugation and inferiority is broken and that the formerly oppressed do not duplicate the oppression of their colonizers. He truly changed the world.

When he passed, I received calls and letters from heads of state, Hollywood artists, professional athletes, Grammy Award winners. The testimonies were so powerful, I was left in awe. Professional athletes used his name on entering the Hall of Fame, actors quoted him when accepting their Oscar, even heads of state asked about him at Commonwealth Heads of Government meetings, according to several Bahamian prime ministers. Some of these leaders visited me personally when they came to the Bahamas on official business because of his impact in their countries.

Many people came to The Bahamas just to visit Bahamas Faith Ministries or to put flowers on his grave. To this day, leaders of countries, prominent pastors, business people, notables from all walks of life routinely visit The Bahamas and the BFM church to speak with me about his impact. Some inform me that their sole reason for being in The Bahamas is Myles Munroe. Business people credit his words with causing their business success. In my travels, the first question border officials often ask me when they see from my passport that I am from The Bahamas is, "Do you know Myles Munroe?"

I surely did know Myles Munroe. We were lifelong friends and brothers; he was my mentor and advisor. We had an incredible journey together for over thirty-five years and throughout this time I was blessed to know this giant and legend up close and personal like very few have; close enough for us to see the other's faults, flaws and gifts. We sharpened each other as iron sharpens iron. He spurred me onto the world stage as he encouraged me to refine my gifts. Together we changed the world. He left us too soon, but he left as he had admonished us to do—he died empty. He caused us to remember his donation rather than his duration.

There once was a man called Myles Munroe. There will never be another like him. The legend is gone, but the legend lives on in everyone who was blessed to cross paths with him.

CHAPTER 1

The Call

November 9, 2014 was a typical day. Nothing was unusual about the Sunday afternoon, other than a scheduled flight to Freeport from Nassau for Dr. Myles Munroe, Dr. Richard Pinder, and other team members to attend the opening of the Global Leadership Conference that night. Two days earlier, Pastor Richard and I were traveling together when the call came in from Dr. Munroe asking both of us if we would make the short twenty-minute flight to Freeport with him. Knowing that he and Dr. Munroe were not supposed to fly together, Dr. Pinder was reluctant at first but indicated that he would go. "I guess it's okay," he remarked, "it's only a twenty-minute flight." I indicated I would not go because I had just purchased tickets for my daughter, Davrielle, and I to fly on a commercial flight the Monday after. Dr. Munroe then asked me for the phone number of our youth pastor Lavard Parks. Lavard Parks and his family—wife, Radel, and son, Jojo—replaced me and my daughter on the flight.

That Sunday morning, we were all in church, and before the sermon Dr. Pinder and I each presented Dr. Munroe with our latest books. Dr. Pinder had just released three books on leadership and I had released my book on leadership lessons for youth. Dr. Munroe welcomed the new projects and stated, "This is the first time I am saying this, but these are my two sons." I was not usually dressed in a suit and tie, but this day I wore a gray plaid sports jacket with a red tie and black pants. Dr. Munroe looked me over and asked me to turn around so everyone could see me. He then said, "You are no more my youth pastor, you are my new pastor." We both laughed and the service continued.

Dr. Pinder, or Pastor Richard as he was widely known, asked me to take him to the airport later that afternoon. I told him I had to go in another direction and would not be home right after service. He replied, "That's okay, I would still like you to take me to the airport. Just call me when you are done." I called him after completing what I needed to do and my wife, Angie, and I proceeded to pick him up. Angie moved to the back seat before we left his house and we headed for the airport. We talked and laughed on the way. When I dropped him off at the private jet airport, I said to him, "I will see you in the morning." I left the airport and headed for home, gazing at the jets as they took to the sky.

I arrived home, had lunch and began to watch a game. I must have dozed off in my family room, because I was suddenly awakened by the sound of phones ringing. Every phone in the house was ringing—the two landlines, my cell phone, my wife's cell phone. I answered my cell phone while my wife answered one house phone, then paused to answer her cell phone while the other house phone kept ringing. Everyone who called was asking the same question: Is it true that Dr. Munroe's jet went down?

Dr. Munroe, pilots and travel team before a flight

I was now fully awake and I told the callers to give me a few minutes to check and see what had happened. The first call I made was to Larry Russell, one of the founders of our Freeport church. He said he needed to do some more checking before giving me a definitive answer. I could not wait for his return call, so I called Captain Pat Rolle, who was the Campus Pastor of our Freeport church and also Director of Civil Aviation with responsibility for flight safety, which covered accidents and crashes.

Sensing the concern in my voice, he did not hesitate, he said very firmly, "N17 is down…and there are no survivors."

In Loving Memory of: Dr. Myles & Ruth Munroe, Dr. Richard Pinder, Pastor Lavard, Radel & Johanan Parks, Farkhan Cooper, Captain Stanley Thurston and Diego DeSantiago

My worst fears now confirmed, I hung my head in disbelief. After a few minutes of fielding calls from all over the world, I realized I needed to do something right away, for the world was descending on The Bahamas seeking answers. I picked up the phone and called our board members and asked them to meet me at the church immediately. The journey to the church was nerve racking, with questions and thoughts circling in my head—*How can this be? Why? What shall we do?* So many questions raced through my mind. There were four original founders of Bahamas Faith Ministries and now only two of us remained. I knew instinctively that the responsibility for Bahamas Faith Ministries rested on the two of us—Pastor Henry Francis and myself.

We arrived at the Diplomat Center (our church building) and found thousands already there. Local leaders, pastors, friends, family members, all had gathered to find out the truth and to support our ministry during this incredible tragedy. As we were heading to the boardroom, Pastor Henry Francis pulled me aside and said, "Dave, it's on you now." It had occurred to me after the first call came in that I would have to take responsibility. That thought stayed with me after I made the calls to the board members, and now it was confirmed. I had no choice; it was on me.

But at that time the outside world neither knew nor understood the background and the dynamics of BFM that had made this choice for me. As a cofounder of Bahamas Faith Ministries, I was well-established locally and internationally with my own local television program. I had a nationally recognized track record on at-risk youth intervention and youth ministry. I was a seasoned entrepreneur and advisor to the Government of The Bahamas on youth matters.

During his succession planning, Dr. Munroe had asked me on several occasions to consider becoming senior pastor when both he and pastor Richard would have transitioned. I was already both youth pastor and assistant pastor of the church. It was his stated desire. I had declined each time the request was made because I was not inclined toward pastoring adults; I was more comfortable launching an organization and ministry that focused on reaching and mentoring troubled youth and on traveling and consulting. It was not a matter of simply declining his request at the time, it was about considering my natural strengths and where I felt I could best serve. I did not consider myself as being disobedient; I had to be honest with myself and about where I felt my best fit would be.

Therefore, I never wanted nor planned nor expected to be in the position I now found myself. But the church faced an unfathomable seismic event, and as one who was there when the baby was born, I knew I could not walk away. It was as if we co founders were all parents of this child and out of the four parents, two were gone. The natural thing was not to look for someone else to take care of the child because it was the responsibility of the parents who remained.

In the Kingdom of God each of us is an ambassador. We have our preferences and desires, but when we sign up for the foreign service, we are never the ones to determine our assignment. I did not choose the assignment; the assignment chose me. An ambassador never tells the King "I will not go where you are sending me"; the ambassador simply carries out the next assignment on the King's orders. There were many unknowns, but I knew I had to lead through the process.

I was always capable and qualified to lead and become a senior pastor, if needed; however, it was just something I never felt I would need to do. I was intimately involved in the church in the background, involved in the planning and decision making. Pastor Richard managed the church and I was his go-to person for vetting decisions. Almost every day we met either in his office or mine. Sometimes, even after meeting most of the day, I would stop by his house on my way home. Pastor Sheena Pinder, Pastor Richard's wife, would remark sometimes, "If you are trying to find Pastor Richard, check with Pastor Dave, he is probably in his office."

BFM had already begun the transition to a new fellowship pastor, which was the position of Dr. Richard Pinder, but not to a new senior pastor, which was the position of Dr. Munroe. The tragedy of November 9 created an unforeseen paradigm shift. None of us thought for a moment that someone other than Dr. Munroe would occupy the office of senior pastor? We all felt he would be with us for a long, long time. There was no indication or speculation that he would be anything but present and leading the vision; so, we had no formal preparation for this event at that time although he had begun discussions about it.

To understand where we were on November 9th 2014 organizationally we have to go back to the beginning. BFM began first with three friends from College, Myles Munroe, Richard Pinder and Dave Burrows having a discussion about a vision for not just a church but a multifaceted non profit that had a church as a component. Dr. Munroe added his brother in law Henry Francis who had been with him during his early ministry with the visionaries and later Jay Mullings who was one of the first members of the church. The vision started with both a local and global intent. We were not formed like a typical church where there was a membership that voted and directed the decisions and direction of the church.

Our legal structure was of a nonprofit corporation and church with a board of governors responsible for policy and decisions. The top officers of the organization at the time were Chairman Dr. Myles Munroe, Vice President Dr. Richard Pinder, Secretary Dr. Dave Burrows, and Treasurer Pastor Henry Francis. Other board members included Merrit Storr, David Knowles, Pat Rolle, Claudine Farquharson, Carl Albury, Kersch Darville, Barbara Lockhart, Arnold Farquharson, Jay Mullings, and Sheena Pinder.

BFM Board Members and BFM friends visit gravesite

That night, those of us who were left gathered as a board and began to discuss the way forward. Even as we dealt with our own grief, we had to respond to the grieving families, the local and international press, our members, and the local Bahamian population. We discussed and deliberated, and after deliberations it was agreed and confirmed that I would take over as the new chairman of the board of Bahamas Faith Ministries International and as senior pastor. I was charged to prepare a statement and address the press shortly thereafter.

We left the board meeting and entered the sanctuary where thousands had gathered trying to comfort one another. There were screams, concerned voices, and a sense of panic and uncertainty. Against this backdrop, I had to confirm that what was reported indeed was true and assure our members that we would make it despite the astounding loss we had incurred. To the best of my ability, I gave assurances that we would get through this great loss. I told our members that the faith that had brought us to where we are would be our hope for the future.

The magnitude of the loss for Bahamas Faith Ministries was unprecedented. We lost our President and Senior Pastor and his wife; our Fellowship Pastor; our Youth Pastor and his wife and children (she was pregnant at the time); our pilots, one of whom had also been a critical board member; and a young man from Los Angeles who had grown up in East Los Angeles and had never left his local community before traveling the world with Dr. Munroe as an interpreter and mentee, eventually becoming like family.

Following my address to the church, we continued to comfort one another. But I had the additional task of communicating with local and global media. ABC, NBC, CNN, CBN, TBN, and many other networks around the world were all seeking answers about the crash and its aftermath. The board members and I returned to the boardroom and I read a prepared statement and fielded questions from the media. I promised the media we would provide more definitive information and guidance after notifying all next of kin. We then left the meeting as friends and followers and embraced each other, and we cried. We tried to comfort one another. It was unbelievable. It was surreal. I walked away recounting Psalm 23 in my head: *"The LORD is my shepherd; I shall not want. He makes me to lie down in green pastures; He leads me beside the still waters. He restores my soul; He leads me in the paths of righteousness For His name's sake. Yea, though I walk through the valley of the shadow of death, I will fear no evil; For You are with me; Your rod and Your staff, they comfort me."*

CHAPTER 2

The History

My connection and relationship to Myles Munroe is a tale of intrigue that can only be described as destiny and a divine connection. We grew up in the same city, but I did not know him. He lived in the heritage community called Bain Town, which some would describe today as a ghetto or the hood. It was hood indeed. We had a nickname for the area, we called it "The Bottom". I frequented Bain Town aka the Bottom as a teenager because of my street connections; I had a gangster friend known as Twadus who lived in the area and I would spend time there doing street business or just hanging out. So, Myles and I may have crossed paths inadvertently, but I am not aware of it happening. I also frequented a nearby area, another hood nicknamed Harlem—after Harlem in New York City—, but the actual name of the street was McQuay. Harlem was one of the most notorious hoods in The Bahamas, and since one of my street mentors Valentine "Kentuck" Huyler, one of the younger brothers of Anthony "Poker" or "24" Huyler, lived there, I hung out there.

During this period of my life, my sisters used to speak about Peter, as Myles was originally known. Later, they talked about Myles who was making waves as a young evangelist and founder of the music group The Visionaires. My sisters were Christians and two were partners with the young Myles, but I had never seen him and had no idea what he looked like. I did not pay attention to anything or anyone church-related. He and his group toured schools, where they played music at assemblies and made altar calls that saw hundreds of students come to Christ. One day, our school announced that Myles and his music group were coming to conduct an assembly. I avoided anything Christian, so I promptly organized a few of my boys to skip assembly and hang out at a local bar and pool room known as The Shoal, and we shot pool and hung out until the coast was clear to return to school. I never had an occasion again to interact with Myles Munroe or even to think about him because we operated in different worlds. I was 100 percent street. He was 100 percent church.

An interesting thing happened a few years later, when I was in college in Madison, Florida, at North Florida Junior College now known as North Florida College that brought us together in an odd way. I still knew very little about him and still had not seen him face to face. In fact I had never seen a photo of him or seen him on television or the newspapers. I had gotten into some big trouble in college and was facing a major legal situation. The police had locked up my friend for something we had done together, and now they were looking for me. I was informed that the penalty I faced could be three years in prison or more. I had not been to church since I was eleven years old, but I was in danger, so

I decided to pray. I remembered that whenever my mother prayed for me, miraculously I would escape dangerous situations. So, with no other viable option that I could think of, I figured I needed to pray to escape the pending problem.

After praying, the popular song "Brand-New World," that Myles's group used to sing, came to mind. I did not know at the time that he wrote the song, I just remembered the words that talked about a new world:

> We don't like the way the world is turning,
> something inside us always yearning,
> yearning for a brand-new world.
>
> People everywhere are so confused;
> leaders don't know just what to do.
> Everybody wants a brand-new world.
>
> Though we send rockets
> to the moon and the stars,
> and though we make trains and ships that go very far,
> and there is not a mountain that man has not climbed,
> yet a brand-new world we could never find.
>
> *'Cause if you want a brand-new world,*
> *you've gotta have a brand-new people.*

And if you want a brand-new people,
you've gotta have a brand-new life.
And if you want a brand-new life,
you've gotta have a brand-new spirit.
And if you want a brand-new spirit,
you've gotta to come to Jesus Christ.

I needed a brand-new world. I called my mother and asked her to send me a copy of the song, and she did. I never explained why. I listened to that song every Sunday morning, even though I still never went to church. Many of those mornings I was high, but I listened, meditating on this brand-new world. I made no connection to Myles nor had any idea that we would ever cross paths. I was in trouble and needed a brand-new world, and this song caught my attention.

While I was in college in Florida, my sister Marilyn was attending Oral Roberts University in Tulsa, Oklahoma. She was the first Bahamian student to attend the school and she was able to persuade Myles Munroe to attend ORU instead of the school he was planning to go to in London. Their friendship continued at ORU. After Marilyn found out about my predicament, she suggested that I come to ORU as it was a better environment and I would be less likely to get into trouble there. She also pointed out that ORU had a top-20 NCAA basketball team because she knew I was a basketball player.

I applied to the school even though I did not qualify. I was looking for something better and I wanted to get out of trouble. I thought both might happen in a more stable environment. So, I outright lied on almost every line of the application. They asked questions about drug use, cohabitation, and church attendance. I had not been to church since I was a young boy, but my mother desperately wanted me to get into the school. She found the pastor who knew me when I was younger, and he provided a recommendation. To my surprise, I was accepted.

Everywhere I went I ended up in trouble, but at ORU I met my brother-in-law Robyn Gool, who ended up leading me to Christ. He was a basketball player also and we spent months all over Tulsa playing basketball. These games led to me accompanying him to Bible studies and eventually to church for the first time in many years. My life was changed by these encounters. I saw something that I had not seen before: a strong man with character and values who was relatable.

Many of my friends were victims of the streets, and I always thought of guys who went to church as soft; so I did not hang around "church boys." But Gool was different. He was strong, he was a great ballplayer, he knew how to talk trash; yet his life was stable and productive. I also saw a different side of Christianity and church. The people in his circle were happy talking about God blessing them. Their church music was upbeat, and I actually enjoyed going to church for the first time in my adult life. His life truly seemed better than mine.

One day, while I was walking across the campus, someone called out to me and asked if I was Dave, Marilyn's brother. I answered yes and he said, "I am Myles Munroe" and proceeded to invite me to hear him speak at a special Vespers service that Sunday in the school's cafeteria. I went to the service and was blown away by the wisdom and insight he displayed. I heard a gospel that made logical sense to me more than before. From that moment we became friends and Myles Munroe became my mentor helping me in my transition from the streets into the Christian life. I met with him often for advice on my journey and he gave recommendations that helped me to grow and stay out of trouble. He even lent me his car when I needed one. I still got into trouble, but this time the result was different: I took the advice and counsel and grew through the process. I was more in the circle of athletes and marginal Christians, so Myles and I were still in different social groups; however, I was growing and evolving, thanks to his mentorship.

Myles graduated a few years ahead of me and went on to do his master's at the University of Tulsa while I completed my education at ORU. After graduating, I was offered a job in Tulsa and initially accepted. After getting my social security card and the job with Youth For Christ Tulsa,

I did an about-face and decided to go home. When I returned to The Bahamas, I began to reach out to my friends and pick them up to play basketball or to attend church. My friends were gangsters, drug dealers, bank robbers, but they listened to me because we were friends from the street days. One or two actually made a significant change. Most wanted to change and were inspired by my **transformation**, but they struggled to leave the streets.

I also began assisting my church, Evangelistic Temple's youth ministry, until one day I got a call that Myles had returned to The Bahamas and wanted me to join him in creating a ministry. Richard Pinder was also a student at ORU and he and Dr. Munroe were friends during their time there. The three of us came together at Myles's in-laws' house and began to discuss the ideas for the ministry. Later, Henry Francis, who was Myles's brother-in-law, came into the picture and the four of us became founders of Bahamas Faith Ministries International.

We were like brothers—Myles, Richard, Henry, and I. We hung out together, went fishing and socialized on a regular basis. Jay Mullings, who joined us shortly after, was the catalyst for our fishing trips and expeditions. Myles would come to my house and have lunch, or I would go to his house. He worked at the Ministry of Education, and I worked next door at the Ministry of Youth. Many days I would go to his office or he would come to my office and we would talk about plans for ministry and the future. We collaborated on projects that I was planning for the Ministry of Youth; he even provided the artwork and drawings for drug- and crime-prevention booklets I was producing. He was an accomplished artist, among his many talents.

We started BFM as a Bible study group and it rapidly evolved into the fastest-growing church in The Bahamas. It was totally different from other churches in worship style, emphasizing praise and worship rather than traditional hymns and it focused on teaching rather than traditional preaching. In the beginning we were all young. I was the youngest of the group, but we were all in our twenties, except Henry Francis and Jay Mullings. As our church grew, more young people began coming to church, including teenagers and children. Seeing the work that I was already doing with young people, Pastor Myles asked me to be the youth pastor for our church. Initially I told him I did not want a title. I was not comfortable with titles and never thought of formal ministry as a career. I resisted all attempts at a formal title until the day he invited me to his office and said, "Dave, you are in denial. I need to ordain you." He asked me a few questions: "Do you preach?" I said yes. "Do you do evangelism?" I said yes. "Do you counsel?" I said yes. He said, "There you have it! You are a pastor. Now let's get this ordination done." I was drafted into service as youth pastor.

Pastor Myles and I spoke almost every day. The ministry began to grow and eventually became nationally recognized. I became recognized nationally as the "Ruffneck Pastor" because of my street background and nontraditional approach to ministry that saw me reaching out to gang members and members of the hip-hop and reggae communities. Many of these young people changed their lives and today are model citizens and leaders in the country.

Several years after the founding of BFM, Dr. Munroe expanded to the world stage. As he began to expand, he invited me to travel with him. Wherever we traveled together—to Baltimore to New York to Los Angeles to New Orleans to Tampa, the list goes on—and no matter how big the stage, he would introduce me and give me ten minutes to speak. These experiences caused me to receive invitations of my own, and eventually I began traveling on my own. He began to write books and encouraged me to write books. He was a global pioneer and trailblazer who opened doors for others. I became a pioneer in youth ministry as I walked along the trail that he cleared for me and began blazing a trail of my own.

Dr. Munroe ultimately became a global icon. His rise from a relatively unknown revolutionary pastor in The Bahamas to a global phenomenon was meteoric. I had a parallel track in youth ministry, although not on the same scale. I began to travel more on my own as our schedules took us in different directions, but we were both changing the world. He soon needed a business infrastructure to manage his global operations. While others within the ministry were managing this for him, after some discussions he decided that my business background and knowledge would serve him well. I founded the Small Business Center in The Bahamas and owned and operated two companies, Megabyte Computers and One Rib Publications. I was appointed vice president and CEO of Myles Munroe International (MMI). This role meant communicating and coordinating engagements and events around the world. It also meant setting up e-commerce and other technology platforms and management systems to attract and manage business with partners around the world. I continued in this vein until Myles Jr. returned to The Bahamas and took over MMI in the mid 2000's, beginning in 2011. A few years earlier, Dr. Munroe had asked me to consider becoming the Senior Pastor as he and Pastor Richard planned to transition to new roles. Dr. Munroe had formed two organizations, Bahamas Faith Ministries International (BFMI) and Bahamas Faith Ministries Fellowship (BFMF) and had begun to preach about passing the baton on. He authored a book about the importance of passing on leadership mantles called "Passing it On" and not taking the baton to the grave. It was during this period that he asked me and I stated that I was not comfortable as a fellowship or senior pastor and preferred the role of youth ministry specialist. I informed him of plans to launch a personal ministry brand much like what he had done with MMI. He eventually accepted that I planned to launch my own brand and began to advise me. One of the first things he said to me was that I should change the name from Dave Burrows Ministries to Dave Burrows International (DBI). He indicated that he would connect me with global contacts, and because some of these contacts were non-Christian, "Ministries" may be an impediment. I made the adjustment and was preparing to officially launch DBI in 2014.

We held several meetings and exchanged emails on the way forward in 2013 and early 2014. In 2013, Charlie Masala, the national director of BFMI, the International Third World Leaders Association (ITWLA) and Myles Munroe International in South Africa, invited me to come to South Africa during their National Youth Month. Dr. Munroe also encouraged me to go to South Africa, for what would be three weeks, to do extensive ministry across the nation, a significant part of which would target youth. I did not accept the invitation initially because I had a conflicting engagement in Alabama.

Dr. Munroe called me into his office and said, "Go to South Africa, this is a pivotal invitation, you can go to Alabama anytime." He said I should call the group in Alabama and renegotiate a new time. I called the group in Alabama and they agreed to postpone the event to a later date. Going to South Africa served as the launching point for my introduction to and expansion in Africa. I thanked him for encouraging me to go to Africa and he remarked that he was proud of me and considered me a trophy of his.

I want to share a few of the emails we exchanged between 2013 and 2014 chronicling our discussions about the future. Forgive the typos; anyone who was close to Dr. Munroe knows that he sent emails all hours of the morning and sometimes forgot to use spell-check.

Mon 6/10/2013 7:35 AM
To:David Burrows (pastordaveburrows@hotmail.com)

Dear Dave,
Greetings from Switzerland! We are having an effective time In Europe.

Thank you for the expression of gratitude. It is good when others return to their leader and says thanks! It encourages us. Thank you!

I am very proud if you and encouraged CHARLIE to invite you to cone to SA.

Represent us well and take good photos to report to the church.

I am proud you and wish you continued success.

See you when you get home.

> Love ya.
>
> Pastor Myles.

You are a trophy to me as a Sr. pastor and I have publically expressed to both locally and internationally.

Dear Dave, Can you please prepare to teach the class tonight from your success book. Suggest the topic:

"THE PRINCIPLE OF SUCCESS -DEFING SUCCESS"

Please confirm.

Thanks.

> Dr. MYLES E. MUNROE
> Chairman: International Third World
> Leaders Association

President: MMI Network

"Transforming Followers in Leaders & Leaders into

Agents on Change"

In 2014, after realizing that I had declined to accept the idea of pastoring since 2013, Dr. Munroe asked if I would postpone the launch of DBI because he had a proposal for me to return to MMI for a period as a senior consultant and advisor. At the time I did not see the position as a good fit and advised him that I preferred to continue plans to launch out on my own while still being a part of the ministry. I stated clearly that I would always be connected to him personally and to BFM. I explained that I saw the DBI vision as complementary to the BFM vision, not detracting from it or competing with it. DBI was what he would term a deployment.

Below are the agenda notes he sent for the January 2014 meeting of Myles Munroe International Bahamas and USA.

NATIONAL BOARD:

Myles Munroe	David Burrows
Chairo Munroe	Beverley Saunders
David Knowles	Merrit Storr
Ethan Moss	Larry Russell
Havard Cooper	

INTERNATIONAL BOARD:

Pepe Ramnath – USA

Charlie Masala – South Africa

Fernando Moreira – Brazil

Darrell Wilson – USA

Yemi Akinsiwaju – England

Margaret Elcock – Trinidad

Jerome Edmondson

Deavra Dauthrey

PROPOSED POSITIONS:

Chairman – M. Munroe

President – Dave Burrows

Chief Operations Officer/Managing Director – xxxxxxxxx

General Administrator – xxxxxxxxxxx

Managers - xxxxxxxx

I had also recently established the Youth and Family Center and entered into a partnership with the Bahamas Government to mentor, counsel and develop troubled youth. Dr. Munroe and I continued discussions and eventually settled on August 2014 as my launch date to be announced at our Kingdom Summit. However, prior to the summit, he asked me to postpone the launch until November. I asked why and he stated that he still needed me in the church. He said he did not know exactly why but he still needed me. We agreed that the launch would then take place in November and began planning for it. Here are some of the email exchanges from that period.

June 7, 2014

Dear Ossie,

Kingdom Greetings from Lagos Nigeria! Just spoke to over 100K people. Amazing. The news from Nigeria is not all bad! My Caribbean Brother it is a joy to hear from you and thank you for acknowledgement of my resignation letter from the P21 Caribbean Advisory Board. I am sure you understand by desire to serve but the reality of many obligations and family priorities demand that manage my time and efforts. Pastor Dave Burrows has a wealth knowledge and will be a great contributor and I hope you will engage him as much as possible.

_____

Launch of Dave Burrows Int. - URGENT FROM PAS MYLES- Followup on Our Recent Meeting - Future Role On Jul 7, 2014, at 10:31 PM, Myles Munroe <myles-munroe@hotmail.com wrote:

Pas. Dave,

I consulted with some of the others and I am planning a full baord meeting next Tuesdsy. Hope you can make arrangement to make it.

Regards,

Dr. Myles Munroe
Chairman

———————————

Myles Munroe 9/20/14

To: DAVE BURROWS

Hi doc, I'm completing a book on leadership for youth and would like to include the five questions, wanted your permission, will make sure and give credit. Let me know, thanks

you got my permission......

My pleasure,
best of success.

Dr. Myles Munroe
Chairman

Looks good Dave. Best of success. Let me know how I can help. Also send me the artwork to post on our Facebook and have then pop it up on our website.

To: DAVE BURROWS

Dave,

This is an excellent idea and one I have unsed over the years but now we can make it a Marketing project, will do.

You teaching on TV sunday was amazing. (relationships) thanks.

In late 2013 or early 2014, BFM's new youth pastor Lavard Parks submitted a proposal to honor my wife and me in the last week of October for our service to the ministry. Dr. Munroe was scheduled to be in South Africa for three weeks at that time and he called me and asked for the event to be postponed so that he could be present. He said there was no way the ministry could honor me and he not be there. He was insistent that a video would not do, he had to be there in person.

Interestingly, my wife approached me a few weeks earlier and asked if I had ever apologized to Dr. Munroe for my response to his invitation to consider serving as fellowship pastor or senior pastor?. His invitation was first presented as an announcement during a board gathering at his house but I was not aware that he was going to make the announcement so in the meeting I objected and said I was not going to accept. He tempered it by saying that I was well equipped and that my wife had the perfect complimentary tools for me to succeed. I told her I never did. I then made an appointment to see him and I apologized. He thanked me and accepted the apology and reminded me that we as a leadership team had been together for over thirty unbroken years, with no church splits or resignations. There were rumors, nonetheless. Some people, both locally and internationally, kept expecting Pastor Richard or me to start a church. There was even a rumor that I had started my own church and taken BFM members with me. People saw my television program and assumed I had started a church.

We agreed to hold the service of thanksgiving and appreciation on Sunday, November 2 and to announce the official launch of DBI during the following week of November 9. We had a great service on November 2, where one of my sons in the ministry Raymond Eneas was the speaker. My wife and I were being released into a new era. At the special luncheon in our honor after the service, we all laughed and fellowshipped and talked about the way forward; Dr. Munroe shared with me details about his trip to Africa. We left the luncheon, both of us excited about the future, for the next Sunday was November 9th.

*From left, Dr. Myles Munroe, Mrs. Ruth Munroe, Mrs. Angela Burrows and
Pastor Dave Burrows at the luncheon honoring Pastor Dave and Angie Burrows on Sunday,
November 2, 2014, at the BFM Diplomat Center*

Dr. Munroe and I conducting an altar call at Youth Alive

Dr. Munroe with "Gangsta" sons. Dave Burrows,
Eric Fox, Raymond Eneas Carlos Reid at event on November 2nd

A Tribute To:
DR. DAVE DAVY-B BURROWS
From The Streets To The World Stage

Over 40 years ago I ran into a young man on the Campus of Oral Roberts University where I too was a student. He introduced himself as a Bahamian, shared how his journey had brought him to ORU and said he had known me from a distance for years. He went on to tell me how impacted he had been by the work I did as a teenager in the 70's with The Visionaires. This began my personal relationship with Pastor Dave Burrows that would last for over 40 years.

Even though Dave Burrows' mother and family were strong believers, his life began on the streets of Nassau in the drug culture where he both sold and used drugs for a number of years. It is clear that Dave is an intelligent and well-educated young man who was smart enough to make good decisions but chose to follow the culture of his peers at the time. However, after a number of encounters with the law the prayers of his mother, Dorcas Burrows were answered. Through his sisters (who worked with me early in the ministry as youth leaders) and his brother-in-law Robyn Gool, David made a decision to submit to the Lord Jesus and follow the God of his mother.

In 1980 when we all returned home to the Bahamas we were all employed by the Bahamas Government: I with the Ministry of Education, Richard Pinder with the Ministry of Social Services and Dave with the Ministries of Social Services and Youth. It was at that time, based on our mutual exposure to Oral Roberts Ministries and the culture of philosophy of the charismatic movement, that I contacted my fellow ORU Graduates, Richard and Dave, to begin a bible study. Naturally, we found fellowship with each other and so began the nucleus of Bahamas Faith Ministries. It is from this point Dave Burrows and his wife Angie became foundation stones of BFM and continue today as major leaders in the vision.

A UNIQUE MAN

Dave brought to the vision and ministry of BFM his vast street culture experience, which at times was a challenge to many of us who were not street-smart. His approach to some aspects of ministry was a manifestation of that unique background. In the early years of the ministry Dave's wardrobe reflected his cool casual lifestyle and his speech, expressions and teaching style were at times coarse and unorthodox. Many times when he was given the opportunity to speak or teach everyone knew they could expect a unique experience that became a trademark of Dave Burrows. It was this unique approach that I identified his special gift to work with youth and in 1985 appointed and ordained Pastor Dave as our Minister and Executive Director of our Youth ministry. Pastor Dave became the first full-time youth pastor in the entire country and the "rest is history".

Dave Burrows and his lovely wife Angie have led the Youth Ministry of Bahamas Faith Ministries International from a small group of excited young people to a major youth movement in the nation. Pastor Dave grew the BFM Youth Alive program of hundreds to "Live Youth" attracting thousands of youth to our annual "Youth Alive" event.

Today I am proud of Pastors Dave and Angie for their accomplishments. Dave has not only matured as a teacher and pastor, but is now a major author with a number of books on youth and family. He has also achieved the status of a youth and family consultant, television host, international speaker and sought-after conference facilitator on the world stage.

Finally, as a member of the Executive Board of Governors of Bahamas Faith Ministries International for the past 35 years, I am deeply indebted and grateful to Dave for his valuable contribution in leadership, management and directorship in guiding the vision of BFM. Dave also served as President of Myles Munroe International which is the business and international outreach of the ministry.

Today I, Ruth and the entire Board of Governors join in with thousands in saluting this great youth leader, husband, father, advisor, businessman and consultant and celebrate Dave and Angie Burrows as youth icons in our generation.

"Dave, continue to dream big, work smart and protect your uniqueness as a Kingdom Ambassador so as to take the message to the next phase of your life."

DR. MYLES AND RUTH MUNROE
Chairman
Bahamas Faith Ministries International (BFMI)
International Third World Leaders Association (ITWLA)
Myles Munroe International (MMI)

Myles Munroe tribute to Dave Burrows Nov. 2nd 2014.

Decisions

On November 10, the morning after the crash, my daughter and I prepared to board our flight to Freeport. She was very close with Dr. Munroe, who always showed her special favor when he traveled to Tulsa, Oklahoma, where she was completing her college studies. Whenever she arrived at an event he was having in Tulsa, he would inform the leaders that she was a VIP and she would be invited to the green room to visit with him. She assisted at his book table and on occasion she and Dr. Munroe would go out with some of her college friends after service for dinner. When my mother died in 2011 he offered his jet to bring her home for the funeral and she accepted, which allowed her the flexibility not to miss classes as she had just arrived at school for the semester.

We sat quietly in the airport in Nassau, then she said to me, "Daddy, I'm scared." I said to her, "I'm scared too, but we don't have the luxury of fear." I didn't realize I had said this to her until sometime later when she reminded me. Everybody was shaken up and there was hesitation and apprehension about anything to do with flying?, but I told her, "I have to go to Freeport because the ministry and the people there need me." We then boarded the flight. So many thoughts were racing through my mind as I contemplated the difficult decisions ahead.

I arrived in Freeport to a distraught gathering of leaders from around the world. Their questions came hard and fast. What would happen at the conference? Would we continue with it? What would happen to the church and ministry? Who will lead? When will the funerals be held? The questions went on and on. The meeting with ITWLA leaders was heart-wrenching. This was a close group of leaders and friends who had been together for many years; we had to comfort each other.

I left the meeting with the ITWLA leaders and headed to the grieving families. Meeting and comforting the grieving families was very difficult, heart-wrenching. I met next with Myles Munroe Jr., Pastor Sheena Pinder, Dr. Pinder's children, and others who were affected. The grace of God was needed, and I had to rely on God's grace to make it through, understanding that my personal pain and loss were exceeded only by the pain and loss of the immediate families, like Charisa and Myles Munroe Jr. who lost both mother and father.

The leaders of ITWLA made the decision to continue the conference, with the belief that it is what Dr. Munroe would have wanted. The conference continued to a successful conclusion and I returned to Nassau with momentous decisions to make. Almost every day for over twenty years, when I entered the Bahamas Faith Ministries parking lot, I met the cars of Dr. Pinder or Dr. Munroe or both there. When I went up the stairs to my office, one or both would be in their office. When I had to make critical decisions, I would stop by one or both of their offices for input and advice. **The day I returned from Freeport, the parking lot was empty, their offices were empty.**

The BFM parking lot when I returned from Freeport

There was no one to talk to. We had been together for over thirty years, and now from this point onward I would have to make every decision without my primary advisors and mentors. I did not have them to lean on. I had tough decisions to make, and I had to make them on my own. It was the most lonely place I had ever been in. But I remembered the words from the book of Joshua: *"[A]s I was with Moses, so I will be with you. Only be strong and very courageous…"*[1]

---

1   Joshua 1:5–7.

I made seven key decisions:

1. **Take ownership and responsibility: accept the assignment**
2. **Provide clear direction to the church**
3. **Protect the ministry from disruption, division and interference**
4. **Promote order and alignment**
5. **Restructure the organization to shift into the new reality**
6. **Communicate vision and plans**
7. **Activate marching orders and redeployment**

DECISION 1 — TAKE OWNERSHIP AND RESPONSIBILITY: ACCEPT THE ASSIGNMENT

I was now assuming the role of Senior Pastor of Bahamas Faith Ministries and succeeding the legend, global icon, once-in-a-generation phenomenal leader, my friend, my mentor, Dr. Myles Munroe. Many voices were calling and offering advice. Members were asking questions. Local and global personalities and entities were inquiring about what would happen to BFM. While I was known to the local congregation and had a global presence as a youth pastor and youth and family specialist and consultant, no one had an idea of how I would function as senior pastor.

I had no experience in that role, but I did have extensive knowledge of the function because of my daily interaction with both Dr. Pinder, who was the fellowship pastor, and Dr. Munroe, the senior pastor. As fellowship pastor Dr. Pinder actually pastored the church because of Dr. Munroe's extensive travel schedule. Every day he and I met to discuss what was happening in the church and he frequently sought my input on critical decisions. In this way, I understood the role but had never wanted to be in the role. Dr. Munroe had previously asked me to consider it and wanted me in the role, but I had been planning a global ministry of my own with continued affiliation with Bahamas Faith Ministries. By instinct and insight, I knew I had no choice: I had to come to terms with accepting the assignment and all that came with it.

This decision was by no means easy. I had avoided officiating funerals, weddings, counseling, and many other duties that came with being senior pastor, but now I had to make a firm decision that I accept the assignment and all that came with it. At one point I did call my brother-in-law Dr. Robyn Gool and expressed my unease. He was pastor of a congregation of over five thousand and was another mentor of mine; so he was able to provide me with valuable insight into how I could function effectively in a role that I had never been in. At the end of the decision-making process I accepted the assignment, without reservation.

DECISION 2 — PROVIDE CLEAR DIRECTION

The realization that there needed to be an immediate shift meant I needed to communicate clearly to the church the way forward and who I was as a leader. **This meant making some immediate tough decisions**.

I let the church and its global followers know that we had "lost the visionary but not the vision." They needed a clear message of assurance and hope, and as the new leader, this message had to come from me. People needed to know we were in good hands. I communicated very clearly *what we would do* and *what our direction would be*. I told them we would "cry while we sharpen our swords." They needed to know we were ready to fight through, that we saw ourselves not as victims but as overcomers. I also coined the phrase "We Remember, We Honor, We Continue" to encapsulate the message that we will never forget our leaders; no matter what, their memory and legacy will remain. We will always honor and never dishonor our former leaders, and it will be our job to continue with strength and purpose into the future. The membership embraced the concept, and we began the journey of moving on.

DECISION 3 — PROTECT THE MINISTRY FROM DISRUPTION, DIVISION AND INTERFERENCE

The membership, for the most part, supported the new leadership and concept, but there were some among us who posed potential problems and I realized I needed to protect the church. I instructed the leaders that no one should be given a microphone during services to say anything without my consent. This was an important position to take because there were individuals who wanted to "prophesy" things that would have completely disrupted the church. We could not afford confusion, so I had to implement controls until such time as everyone was settled.

I allowed no outside interventions or input to take place without my approval. This too was an important policy position because there were laypeople and professionals within the local community who were trying to get us to follow their protocol on grief counseling, including holding a service where everyone would bring teddy bears and other items as points of contact as they cried. These professionals had contacted some of my leaders and these leaders had given consent for something like this to happen, but I could not allow the world to tune in and see God's people looking lost and confused, holding teddy bears and crying.

In the week following the crash, over 900,000 people tuned in to our livestream on a Sunday morning looking for answers and hope. I could not afford to broadcast a chaotic scene to the world. I knew I had to be decisive and ensure that our global family understood that we would recover. I communicated that we would have the *same vision but a different leader*. Dr. Munroe was gone, and I could not replace him; I could only follow the vision according to my skill set, personality and spiritual insight.

DECISION 4 — PROMOTE ORDER AND ALIGNMENT

I also let people know that order and alignment were key to our future success. We could not afford to be divided, and people who were seeking prominence under Dr. Munroe would not be allowed to use this period to obtain it. Several members presented themselves, intimating that Dr. Munroe had spoken to them about having a more prominent role or about speaking in the church. I let everyone know that we would have order and I would advise who fit where, and that no one should use Dr. Munroe's name to gain position or favor.

I cautioned the ones whom I did allow to speak that if they were not respectful of their time they would be nudged and face discipline or be asked to step away. My resolve was tested in the beginning, but as soon as persons saw I meant business, everyone else fell in line. Mindful that the younger generation is less tolerant of extended services, especially in the absence of the magnanimity of Dr. Munroe, I developed and introduced a new service structure that significantly reduced the duration of services. I encouraged all members to find their place in the vision and submit to the new leadership and not try to determine their own roles. Everyone had a role to play, and the leadership team led by me would make the decisions. All we needed was for people to be willing and to cooperate. There was enough work for everyone, but everything needed to be done decently and in order.

DECISION 5 — RESTRUCTURE THE ORGANIZATION TO SHIFT INTO OUR NEW REALITY

With Dr. Munroe no longer in the picture, our organization needed to shift. He had a massive global presence and generated income that sustained the existing infrastructure, but we did not know what the future would look like without him. He was the driving force for our global footprint, and with him gone, it would likely mean a shift to a more locally based ministry and church. I had been traveling and I planned to continue to travel, but the scale of my influence was far less than his. I had to make difficult budgetary decisions.

Dr. Munroe attracted income through his global ministry which required staffing and infrastructure. Now that he was gone, adjustments had to be made to account for a different financial environment. We also lost key members of our board of governors, and we needed to put new leaders in their place. With this perspective in mind, I secured the commitment of Mr. Ethan Moss and Dr. Kendal Major, who were added to the board.

I was the main business voice on the previous board, but now we had a prominent, seasoned and influential businessman as a part of our team in Ethan Moss. Dr. Major would prove to be a critical addition also as he was Speaker of the House of Assembly and a prominent national figure who was close to the seat of power in the country. These additions strengthened our board and positioned us for the future as a knowledgeable and diversified board.

I also restructured our church council, which is the second highest governing group in the church. I added younger leaders and changed meeting times and structure. I had been to these council meetings on a regular basis, but when I presided over my first meeting and looked out into the crowd, I realized the group was largely made up of older people. I told myself that I must change this and add younger leaders to understudy those currently in place to ensure that we transition successfully. We also made legal adjustments to ensure compliance with national laws, and we put in protective measures to ensure there would be less guess work in the future. The board of governors would have access to clear policies.

DECISION 6 — COMMUNICATE VISION AND PLANS

People came to me and asked what the new vision for the ministry would be. I explained that there would be no new vision; the vision that we were founded on remains the vision. What there would be is refinement of the vision to account for new leadership and a new season. We would also present adjusted plans because some of the plans in place required that Dr. Munroe be present. For example, we had plans on the drawing board for a physical location of a brick-and-mortar leadership institute. Most of the people were projected to attend the institute would have been attracted by the opportunity to engage with Dr. Munroe himself. He was to be the main facilitator and the driving force. The institute would not be the same without him present; so, we had to look at the possibility of developing an online school using his materials, rather than constructing a building.

When you are building a house, you first prepare a vision of the house, a set of architectural drawings or plans. You adjust plans but you do not cancel an established vision. I was there when the baby was born. I helped to formulate the vision. Now, for the first time, I was thrust into the lead role of executing the vision. I had to consider all the current factors and adjust plans accordingly. Some people were offended that we decided not to construct a building for the leadership institute and they went so far as to say we had to build it because Dr. Munroe said he was going to build it. I explained the new dynamics and prayed as Jesus did: *Father, forgive them, for they know not what they are speaking about or doing.* [2]

---

2   Luke 23:34.

DECISION 7 — ACTIVATE MARCHING ORDERS AND REDEPLOYMENT

The new dynamics meant that some people would have to be redeployed. BFM consisted of Bahamas Faith Ministries International, Bahamas Faith Ministries Fellowship, and Myles Munroe International. We were in the process of separating Myles Munroe International from Bahamas Faith Ministries prior to his death, but it was now imperative to accelerate the process. Nonetheless, some responsibilities would be shifted, some staff would be released, some would be transferred from one entity to another, and some would remain as they were.

The process can be likened to a war strategy, where troops are deployed to the war front and once that battle is over, they are redeployed to a new arena. I had to do an assessment of roles and resources and present new marching orders based upon our new structure. Some individuals who were previously not engaged at all were engaged and given marching orders based on the adjustments we had made. Change was hard for some while others embraced this new opportunity. I admonished everyone that we had to be firm and focused for the new season. Thankfully, there was tremendous buy-in and we were on our way with very few casualties.

BFM 2015-16

CHAPTER 4

The Transition

Transition is the process or a period of *changing* from one state or condition to another. Bahamas Faith Ministries was transitioning from one leader to another, from severe trauma to transformation in a new day and a new era. The challenges were great, but the transition had to begin. I had to do a critical analysis of where we were and begin the process.

In some ways it was a seamless transition. Wherever I traveled in the world, people marveled at how easy the transition seemed. While everything worked out fine and appeared to have been smooth sailing, the transition to new leadership was by no means easy; there were significant obstacles and challenges. In the background were issues—miscommunications, misunderstandings, and any number of things—that could have derailed the process.

DO WE HAVE THE RIGHT LEADER?

Just days after assuming leadership, I sent out a communication to my personal mailing list which was then accidentally sent to the entire BFM global mailing list by our employee responsible for sending eblasts. Some individuals interpreted this eblast as evidence I was using the ministry's list for my personal gain. It was a simple mistake, yet enough people quickly formed opinions about me and concluded that I was attempting to erase Dr. Munroe to co-opt the ministry as my personal empire. This was ludicrous, but in times of turmoil a lot can get lost in translation, and a lot was.

I could not respond to all the rumors and drama because to do so would have pulled me away from critical transition tasks and communications. Some members questioned if I was appointed too soon. Others wondered if Dr. Munroe had selected Pastor Kersch Darville to become senior pastor. It had been announced before the tragedy that Pastor Darville would become fellowship pastor and some members did not know the difference between that position and senior pastor. Outsiders also did not know the difference, and some of them began to circulate rumors on social media that I had executed an illegal takeover. When my office adjusted the brand colors of the church's stationery, individuals claimed that I had changed the colors to my favorite colors. There was a group, not even connected to the ministry, preparing to go on air at a local radio station to spread misinformation. Thankfully, an influential national figure who also was about to go on air contacted me to say, "Dave, do you know these people, and did you sanction them to speak about this issue?" I told him no, I did not, and he promptly told the station owner not to let them on the air. Some global followers and supporters of BFM assumed that Dr. Mun- roe's children would assume leadership of the church and some of them began to post on social media that I had "stolen" the church. People who knew nothing about BFM or BFMI were asking who I was and where had I just come from to take the church from Dr. Munroe's family. I never responded to these claims because the decision-makers that mattered knew the truth. His heirs and survivors were fully engaged in their professional pursuits and were administrating Myles Munroe International which was a separate entity from the church. Persons on the outside who did not understand the structure of the church made assumptions without knowledge, which can occur in times of uncertainty. This was a non issue perpetuated by lack of knowledge.

I was also informed that meetings were being held by individuals outside the country, including some of Dr. Munroe's mentees and associates, to stop me from "stealing the ministry." Sadly, these people lacked knowledge or understanding of the dynamics and history of the ministry and lacked any authority to render an opinion. So, their effort was shut down after one of our board members got wind of it. The board member informed them that we as a ministry knew exactly what we were doing and that it was not by accident nor by pretense nor by any subversive means that I had been appointed. Our Board of Governors who comprised the highest governing body of BFM decided as a team to take swift decisive action to ensure that what usually happens in transitioning churches did not happen to us.

Bahamas Faith Ministries is governed by a board of governors and the board makes decisions on the future of the church. Our organizational governance had no provision for transition outside of the board's review and decision. Many board members were aware that Dr. Munroe had desired me to lead the ministry and that it was I who did not accept the position at the time. He approached me a second time in 2013 via one of the board members; I respectfully said no to the board member, and we laughed about it. He later persuaded Dr. Munroe that I might have changed my mind and volunteered to approach me again. Dr. Munroe informed the board member that he had already spoken to me. "But," said Dr. Munroe, "that is your friend; so if you want to, you can speak to him."

The board of governors, church council and most of the leadership team clearly understood the leadership dynamics. Nonetheless, there were some who behaved as if they did not and created some minor tension. But because all the critical voices knew the truth, it was not difficult to settle the issue, which rested on the fact that I was not a novice by any means. In addition to being a cofounder of BFM, I was established on the global stage as a consultant and advisor to churches and denominations. I was the leader of several leadership entities both locally and internationally, and I served on the boards of BFM, the International Third World Leaders Association, the Global Youth Ministry Network, and the Christian Youth Leaders network, to name a few.

I was a self-made entrepreneur and owner of two companies, Megabyte Computers and One Rib Publications. I had been youth pastor for over twenty-five years. I was a nationally recognized youth specialist having chaired the Bahamas National Youth Advisory Council on three occasions. I was a serial innovator and trendsetter in youth ministry in The Bahamas.

I was also Vice President of Myles Munroe International, communicating with major global ministries on a regular basis. I flew on his private jet to meetings with major global figures and was the go-to person designing business plans, PowerPoint presentations and communications, and at times authoring papers for critical meetings between Dr. Munroe and major corporate executives and business partners, and even the Prime Minister of The Bahamas. I was fully prepared though not planning for the eventuality. None of us ever expected Dr. Munroe to be gone; it seemed he would live forever, or at least for a long time. But my skillset and experience meant that if required, I could tackle the assignment without trepidation.

CAN WE TRUST THE PROCESS?

Some churches that have had to transition resolved their leadership impasse by having members vote. In some of these cases, the vote led to church splits, long legal battles, or severe acrimony and turmoil that involved lockouts and even physical altercations. At BFM we were able within one week to complete the plan for the way forward and announce new leadership. We enunciated the vision and plans and rallied everyone around the vision.

Once it was clear that we had a plan and knew exactly where we were going, the church actually began to grow. In the first year we grew by 15 percent. Another local church that had lost its founder due to retirement lost 600 out of 800 members. Another church ended up in court with extended legal battles, lockouts, and near-physical altercations. We were able to continue successfully without incident. We focused on our vision and core message and redeployed members according to their strengths. We made the right decision and used the right process, and the proof was in how the church stayed together and grew despite the catastrophic loss we had experienced.

We simply ran with the vision that Dr. Munroe had clearly enunciated and reiterated year after year: "We transform followers into leaders and leaders into agents of change and our primary message is the message of the Kingdom, the only gospel that Jesus Himself preached."

WILL WE REMEMBER?

I also insisted on honoring Dr. Munroe and Dr. Pinder. "We Remember, We Honor, We Continue" was not just a slogan, it was a commitment to remember where we came from and to continue in the same spirit our founders would have wanted. Some people did not understand that Dr. Myles Munroe and Dr. Richard Pinder were not casual acquaintances to me. These were my brothers. If anyone was hurting, it was me. I lost my lifelong friends. Like any brothers, along the way and over the years we had issues and disagreements, but make no mistake about it, we were brothers. I could not for a minute let outside detractors and misinformed individuals interfere with the vision continuing as it should.

In the year before he died, Dr. Munroe called the original group together at his house and stated that he wanted us to return to the way we were in the beginning, where we visited each other's homes, went fishing together, and spent time together. He spoke of wanting our children to become closer to the vision and become more involved. He said he wanted my daughter to become youth pastor; he wanted to see his children become more involved in the ministry as well if they desired it. He wanted the foundation that had built us into who we are to remain strong as we prepared to transition into new roles.

I made sure my friends received proper honor. I petitioned the Bahamas Government to change the name of Carmichael Road, where BFM was located, to Myles Munroe Boulevard. The government resisted this appeal so we could not move forward with it. We did change the name of the road leading to the church to Richard Pinder Drive and we changed the name of the church's building from simply Diplomat Center to Myles E. Munroe Diplomat Center.

I was deeply hurt by what some people were insinuating about my motives, but I knew, and those close to the ministry knew, the truth of my relationship with Dr. Munroe and Dr. Pinder. I had to pray as Jesus did: "Father, forgive them, for they know not what they do." Probably the hardest thing I had to do in my life thus far was to open the local newspapers to see their names and images in the obituary section. I cried for several days. A few days later it struck me that I was sending out emails as usual to Myles Munroe and Richard Pinder. Realizing that there would be no answer, I accepted that I had to delete them from my mailing lists. I could not do it. I asked my daughter to do it for me. I thank God that through it all, the strength of the vision and the strength our relationship prevailed over everything.

Naming Richard Pinder Drive, renaming Myles Munroe Diplomat Center.

CHAPTER 5

Succession Planning I

To understand why BFM was successful in its transition and succession, we must understand the principles of succession. But first, what is succession? According to Websters Dictionary:

"Succession is the act of assuming a title or the responsibility of a position right after the person who had that title has retired, left, died or is no longer able or allowed to have it".

It is important to note that succession is different from replacement".

You can succeed someone, but you can never replace another human being, especially a once-in-a-generation, phenomenal leader and global icon. Nor should you seek to replicate another human being; even identical twins are not replicas of each other. God used a single unique mold for each person He created, and when that person is gone, the mold is gone forever, never to be reused. Therefore, every leader is unique, a unique individual and personality. Since we can neither replace nor replicate a leader, it follows that succession must be planned and executed in the right context. Unfortunately, the importance of succession is overlooked by organizations.

Consider these facts:

- Only 10 percent of small business owners have a formal, written succession plan; 38 percent have an informal, unwritten plan; the remaining 52 percent do not have any succession plan at all. (The BEI 2016 Business Owner Survey)
- Nearly two-thirds of family businesses don't have a documented and communicated succession plan.[3]
- Only 35 percent of small businesses have started the process of succession planning, and of this group, only 8 percent have a complete written plan, according to 2022 research from MassMutual.
- Only about 30 percent of family businesses survive into the second generation, 12 percent are still viable into the third generation, and only about 3 percent of all family businesses operate into the fourth generation or beyond. [Family Business Institute)
- Less than 50 percent of churches have a succession plan (Barna group **Leadership Aug 6, 2019**).

Where no succession plan is in place, the likely results are:

- Church splits: a successor was not identified

---

3   Price Waterhouse US Family Business Survey 2023.

- Church wars: legal battles, repossessions (In one case, the pastor's wife's car was repossessed when she sent it to the dealer for servicing.)
- Delays: church ends up in limbo and indecision with no pastor, or a contested reign of the new pastor
- Uncertainty: members are not sure who to follow, do not know what the vision is going forward.

It is critical for every church (and business, for that matter) to have:

- Systems: a way of operating that transcends personalities and can be passed on seamlessly.
- Provisions: written information and resources that are available in the event a transition does take place.
- Organizational charts and job descriptions: to prevent ambiguity about roles and functions.
- Financial policies and structure: to show that finances are professionally set up and personal and church finances are separated, along with clear instructions on what happens financially if a founder retires or passes away.

With that said, in this and the next chapter I will share several principles or first rules of succession and transition.

Principles of Succession and Transition

A principle is "a rule; a law or a law of nature; a fundamental assumption; a moral rule; the main way of doing something." [Merriam Websters dictionary] "Something established as a standard or test, for measuring, regulating, or guiding conduct or practice. A principle is a general and fundamental truth that may be used in deciding conduct or choice: to adhere to principle." [Merriam Websters dictionary]

Sometimes we equate succession with replacement. Succession is not replacement. Since no one can be replaced, we must focus on how to "follow" or succeed a leader? The question I faced was how do I follow a phenomenal leader, a global icon, and a once-in-a-generation transcendent personality?

Principle 1 - YOU ARE A SUCCESSOR NOT A REPLACEMENT

The first key is to ensure people know you are not the replacement. A friend who was a youth pastor of a famous church informed me that his senior pastor would never tell the congregation when he was traveling because many members would not come to church if the pastor was not there. If they showed up on a Sunday morning and someone other than the pastor was introduced, the members would react with anger or sorrow. On such Sundays, the youth pastor had to be on point, focused and phenomenal, otherwise he would be rejected.

Imagine being the person who has to rise to the occasion and take the podium after Dr. Myles Munroe. Exactly. It is an intimidating task. This was the task I faced, and although daunting, I knew I was ready. I let everyone know I am not the replacement; I am not here to attempt to duplicate Dr. Munroe's words or personality. I am here to run the next leg of the race with the unique skills, talent and insight resident in me. I made it clear from the very first sermon that I was different and that I was there not to duplicate Myles Munroe but to carry on with the vision that I helped birth and develop. Thank God I was not a novice or unfamiliar with the vision. I knew it would be a challenge, but from the first Sunday, members began to say they felt the ministry was in good hands.

Principle 2 - THE VISION NOT THE VISIONARY IS LASTING

The most important component of successful succession is *vision*. Success begins with a vision. Scripture tells us in Habakkuk 2.1–3:

> I will stand my watch
> And set myself on the rampart,
> And watch to see what He will say to me,
> And what I will answer when I am corrected.

> Then the LORD answered me and said:

> "Write the vision
> And make it plain on tablets,
> That he may run who reads it.
> For the vision is yet for an appointed time;
> But at the end it will speak, and it will not lie.
> Though it tarries, wait for it;
> Because it will surely come,
> It will not tarry."

The significant charge is to write the vision down and make it plain, or clear, so that those who come after may read it and run with it. Bahamas Faith Ministries became what it was and is because of the vision. If you are reading this book, you are here because of that vision. Vision is powerful, so powerful, the Bible tells us, that people will perish without it.

To ensure success we must ensure that people know the vision and follow that vision and not a personality. A vision can transcend generations while a personality will not. Each personality has a limited shelf life. We all will die, and we do not know exactly when. Jesus left earth more than two millennia ago, but He left a vision in place that the disciples followed and that we are still following today. There have been a series of runners, running with the original vision in different forms.

If an organization is personality based, it dies with the personality. Dr. Myles Munroe (and you and I) cannot ever be replaced, but we can be successors. We can be successors either individually or collectively. Jesus did not have an individual successor; He selected twelve because He knew there was no one person who could represent Him effectively. No one possessed the qualities to survive the demand or expectation of following Jesus. Jesus was succeeded collectively thanks to a clear vision and that vision was about the Kingdom of God, which is what Jesus preached and reiterated. We remember His words:

> *"Your kingdom come. Your will be done / On earth as it is in heaven"* (Matthew 69–10).

"Seek first the Kingdom of God and His righteousness" (Matthew 6:33).

"Except a man be born again, he cannot see the kingdom of God" (John 3:3 KJV).

His vision was for the Kingdom to manifest itself on earth through His disciples and all those who would follow.

According to a study in the *Wall Street Journal*, "Students of leadership say that companies that navigate the transition most successfully are those that embed the founder's values in the organization and groom multiple generations of leaders".

We must be principle based to preserve an organization and vision in the absence of the founder or leader. Success and succession usually revolve around the initial vision. To transition effectively you must have the original vision and blueprint. It is important to emphasize vision because visions extend beyond lifetimes and visions can survive personalities. Once the vision is plain, it has to be continually communicated and reinforced, especially in the face of change. Never take communication of the vision for granted.

I remember having a conversation with Dr. Munroe after a meeting with church leaders where he spent over an hour talking about the vision. I asked him why he spent so much time telling the same group of people about the vision when he had done it so many times before. His response was, "Never assume the people who work for you understand the vision or have bought into it. Even if they do understand it, they need to be constantly reminded, or they will lose sight of the vision and stray away." From that moment I learned a lesson that I have always used since: Never take communication of the vision for granted or assume key people understand the vision.

One of the people who operated on this principle is the founder of Apple Computers, Steve Jobs. He was a once-in-a-generation leader whose vision was to be creative and innovative and to lead the marketplace rather than follow trends. He reiterated to his staff and customers that Apple "thinks differently." Think Different was prominently displayed in all their ads or presentations. Their branding was Think Different.

The result was a company that kept innovating and introducing products that did not look like the products of other companies. There were hundreds of computer brands that all looked alike—black or gray boxes with standard shapes and architecture. Apple, on the other hand, was the first to popularize the mouse, all-in-one computers, computers with colors and different shapes, the iPod for music, the iPad, and the iPhone smartphone, to name a few. Apple was the creator of apps, which later became standard on smartphones.

Steve Jobs was fired from his own company due to internal conflicts. The board brought in a CEO by the name of John Scully, who came from the corporate world. Apple was not a suit-and-tie company. Steve Jobs always dressed casually. He created a culture based on his vision. Apple was not a standard box company; it looked different. But under John Scully, Apple went from "Think Different" to "Think Same." Apple's products began to look the same as others', and with Apple usually being higher priced, there was nothing to attract consumers. The company almost went out of business. The comeback for Apple came when the original visionary returned to the company, leading to some of its most iconic innovations.

Remember that the vision is bigger than the visionary. Visionaries have an appointed time, but visions do not, they can be perpetual. Jesus constantly repeated the vision to His disciples for three years. He constantly spoke of the Kingdom of God. His famous refrains were to seek first the Kingdom, be born again to see the Kingdom. He referred to the Kingdom as being like the pearl of great price, the mustard seed, the field that would cause one to sell everything to get it. A vision is so powerful that men can be dead for more than fifty years and people continually refer to their vision: "I have a dream" is still remembered as the words of Martin Luther King Jr., who was the visionary behind civil rights and racial equality in the United States and eventually the globe.

For those who associated with or were influenced by Dr. Myles Munroe, his mantra and motto is etched in our minds: "Transforming followers into leaders and leaders into agents of change." This was his overriding vision. We remember the words even if we never met or befriended the author. In succeeding him, if I had shifted to some other vision, I may have caused confusion among the church and its followers. But I did not and could not shift, for I was a part of the original vision; I did not come along and join the vision. This was my mantra and my motto too.

BFM is also a Kingdom message-driven church. This was ingrained in the leadership and reiterated often to the membership. I recall a member coming to me and asking when we are going to move on from Kingdom teaching because Dr. Munroe is no longer here. I explained to the individual that the Kingdom message is not a fad. The message of the Kingdom is what Jesus preached, nothing else. The message of the Kingdom embodies faith; it is grace; it is prayer; it is the Holy Spirit. Even church itself is Kingdom because the church is the entity charged with introducing the Kingdom on earth. All of these—faith, grace, prayer, Holy Spirit, church—are what we call components of the Kingdom, and if we examined the overriding message of Jesus, we would see that He came to earth to establish not a church or religion but the Kingdom. The church happens to be the agency charged with causing the Kingdom to be manifest on earth.

Principle 3 - SUCCESSION CAN BE PLANNED, CIRCUMSTANTIAL OR BOTH

Succession can be the result of varying eventualities. Succession can be planned and orchestrated deliberately, or it can be circumstantial. It can also be a combination of both. There was planning in the background and the principles of succession were being employed by Bahamas Faith Ministries, but the resultant succession was circumstantial. If not for the unique circumstances of the November 9, 2014 tragedy, I likely would not have succeeded Myles Munroe.

The sudden departure of not one but two of the founders demanded that I shift course in the face of the existential demands thrust on Bahamas Faith Ministries. The magnitude of our loss highlights why leaders must focus on applying principles rather than a template. Templates do not take into account unusual circumstances and events. Nonetheless, there is no excuse for not having a plan. A plan needs to be in place. If everything goes according to plan, the succession happens as planned. If circumstances arise where there is death, sickness, moral failure, or someone decides they do not want to be associated with the church or organization for any number of reasons, both eventualities are covered. In my case, I was the one who had been prepared and equipped, even though it was not my plan to be the successor. Circumstances changed dramatically, and I ended up having to change course for the sake of a vision that I cofounded and was intricately involved in for over thirty years.

Principle 4 - THERE IS NO ONE-SIZE-FITS-ALL TEMPLATE
There are many successful examples of succession in business and the church, and this fact clearly indicates that there is no one-size-fits-all template. Let's look at a few of these successes.

- **Lakewood Church**. Joel Osteen was neither identified nor prepared as successor. He was a behind-the-scenes media personality who shunned the limelight and was averse to public speaking. His father was a fiery preacher, but Joel, he was a humble, simple communicator who showed minimal emotion. Yet his leadership caused the vision of Lakewood Church to explode to levels his father had never seen.

- **Walmart**. After the passing of its founder Sam Walton, Walmart fluctuated. None of the Walton children emerged as the go-to successor. Walmart continued on the strength of the vision of its founder Sam Walton through ebb and flow. The Walton family succeeded him collectively without a clear successor.

- **Crenshaw Christian Center**. Frederick Price Jr. succeeded his father, Frederick Price Sr. He too followed a legend and there are challenges with following a legend. Fred Jr. is an excellent teacher of the Word, but the church struggled somewhat when compared to its glory days under his father. The church and ministry now continue with some success, but it is not the same.

- **The Walt Disney Company**. When founder Walt Disney passed away, there was an initial decline in the company. No individual successor drove Disney's rebound. The vision of the founder was the guiding light that steered its successive CEOs. They have had varying degrees of success, but the vision is what has caused the company to succeed.

- **Microsoft**. Microsoft declined and became stagnant after its founder retired from the company. The company evolved and refined its vision, with other cofounders steering it in new directions. The original vision remained but plans and strategies changed based upon marketplace conditions and global trends.

- **Honda Motor Company.** Honda saw its greatest innovations after the death of its founder. New leadership spurred new ideas and reshaped Honda into an expanded version of the original company leading to groundbreaking innovations.

The Bible tells us that many are the plans in a man's heart, but the Lord's purpose will prevail:

> Listen to counsel and receive instruction,
> That you may be wise in your latter days.
>
> There are many plans in a man's heart,
> Nevertheless the LORD's counsel—that will stand. — Proverbs 19.20–21

Principle 5 - PASS ON THE VISION NOT YOUR WARDROBE

In the biblical story of Saul and David, David was forced initially to wear Saul's wardrobe in battle. If he had continued in Saul's wardrobe, we never would have seen the real David. He would have been defeated because Saul's clothes were not a fit for David. When David put away Saul's wardrobe and wore what fit him, he succeeded.

Joel Osteen succeeded his father and caused the vision to expand because he wore his own clothes. Whatever one may think of him theologically or otherwise, he wore his own clothes and walked in his own shoes and found success in growing the church. Principles are the most important thing. There is nothing wrong with having a template, but principles are more important than a template.

One day, a member came to me and said, "You have big shoes to fill." I knew what he meant, but I told him I would never attempt to fill Dr. Munroe's shoes. **I can walk in his footsteps, but I cannot fill his shoes.** After all, I wear size 12 shoes; his shoes were significantly smaller. If I put on his shoes they would not fit. I am speaking figuratively, of course, but I believe you get the message. I cannot wear another man's clothes. I will walk in his footsteps wearing my own wardrobe and my own shoes. My predecessor is no longer here to give advice, so I have to do my job according to who I am. When David got comfortable in his own clothes, he was able to defeat Goliath, although to many watching, his approach did not make sense and was unorthodox.

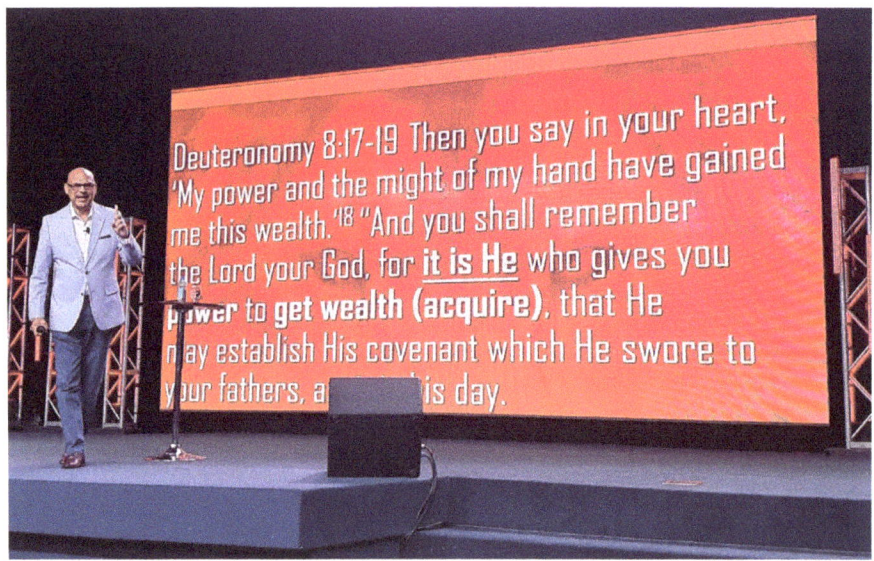

CHAPTER 6

Succession Planning II

Principles of Succession and Transition

In the previous chapter, I shared five principles of succession and transition:

Principle 1 - YOU ARE A SUCCESSOR NOT A REPLACEMENT

Principle 2 - THE VISION NOT THE VISIONARY IS LASTING

Principle 3 - SUCCESSION CAN BE PLANNED, CIRCUM-STANTIAL OR BOTH

Principle 4 - THERE IS NO ONE-SIZE-FITS-ALL TEMPLATE

Principle 5 - PASS ON THE VISION NOT YOUR WARDROBE

Here are the remaining principles.

Principle 6 - IDENTIFY THE GIFTS AND TALENTS OF KEY PEOPLE

Visionary leaders must have the eyes of a coach. Watch your team to determine the best fit of each of the players. I used to coach basketball, and at the very first practice I would ask the players to take a ball and run up and down the court. That drill alone told me who would be my guards, forwards, and centers, and who had ballhandling skills and who did not. This knowledge allowed me to position each player correctly and steer him in the direction of his strengths. Dr. Munroe did this very well. He not only steered me in the direction of my strengths, he encouraged me to refine my skills for greater impact.

Early in ministry I was known as the "Ruffneck Pastor." I was rough in my speech, my delivery and my appearance. It worked well among gang members and youth from the streets. It did not work well with some pastors and leaders in other communities; some found the rough speech offensive. Dr. Munroe pulled me aside one day and said, "Dave, what you are doing is good and effective on the streets. If you ever want to expand your reach you have to refine your gift to make it more palatable on all levels." He told me I have the talent to reach from the "outhouse to the Whitehouse" and if I refined my gift, more people would call on me in places I have never been. Sure enough, as I refined my gift, I began to get calls from all over the world leading to a new era and a shift in my ministry. He helped to position me for success based upon what he saw of my gifts, talents and skills.

Principle 7 - EXPECT DUPLICATION OF VISION AND VALUES BUT NOT PERSONALITY OR METHODOLOGY

Expect duplication of vision and values. Do not expect duplication of personality or methodology. The Bible says to write down the vision— not write down the methodology or the personality traits. Vision and values can be translated outside of personality. Personality and methodology are linked to a person and a season and do not necessarily need to be duplicated. For example, the vision of our youth ministry was focused on reaching young people, discipling them and producing leaders. My methodology as the "Ruffneck Pastor" was based upon my personal background and experience. The next youth pastor did not come from the streets in the same way that I did, and he may not have been able to relate to troubled youth in the same way that I did. What he needed to do was to lead according to his personality using the methodology that works for him.

Jesus told his disciples to go into all the world and preach the gospel.[4] He was confident that they would be smart enough to know how to do it in their environment. He did not leave a method, He left principles. Apostle Paul said he became all things to all men in order to win some.[5] This means he adjusted methods based upon the audience but did not change the message. The message is the same, the vision is the same, but the methodology changes. We live in a time of great technological ad-

---

4   Mark 16.15.
5   1 Corinthians 9.19–23.

vancement, where seismic shifts are occurring from one year to the next. If we use what worked ten years ago, we will hamper our effectiveness.

Dr. Munroe and I were both very strong personalities in our own way. He was an outgoing, people-driven, ebullient personality. I am somewhat reserved by nature. I have always been quiet and rather shy of public attention and interaction. However, I can be comfortable in crowds. I know how to operate with crowds and have no issue engaging and communicating. Dr. Munroe used to remain after church and speak to members for hours. I, on the other hand, would greet members after service and then leave within thirty minutes. Neither approach is wrong, but if I tried to be Dr. Munroe, I would be uncomfortable and less effective as a leader.

Principle 7 - RECOGNIZE YOUR OWN FALLIBILITY AND FLAWS

No matter how great leaders may be, they all have flaws. Recognize your own fallibility and mortality. Failure to recognize your own flaws can lead to overconfidence and a sense of invincibility. It can also cause you to believe you are needed more than you are and to postpone planning for succession. When you recognize your own flaws and mortality, you accept that although you are important, you are ultimately dispensable. It is best to plan with this eventuality in mind rather than allow yourself to come to the point where you are forced out.

I recognized what Dr. Munroe's strengths and weaknesses were. I recognized his gifts and abilities. I knew there were things he did exceptionally well and others that he did not. In the same way that he had strengths and weaknesses, so did I. My wife pointed out my weaknesses as we progressed, and rather than argue, I chose to work on my weaknesses and flaws to become a better version of myself. I had to recognize where I made mistakes and what I could have done better. When I know I have offended someone, or it is pointed out to me that I have, I apologize and seek to correct the situation. The more you are willing to acknowledge and address your weaknesses and flaws, the easier it will be to transition effectively.

Principle 8 - ASSIST POSSIBLE SUCCESSORS IN DEVELOPING AND REFINING THEIR GIFTS

One of the great lessons I learned from Dr. Myles Munroe was the distinction between deployment and employment. Deployment is the act of moving something or someone into a strategic position or a position of readiness, or the condition of being in such a position **(Merriam Webster Dictionary).** When you are surrounded by gifted and talented individuals, you tend to employ them to work for you as employees. Dr. Munroe's philosophy was to deploy and not employ key people.

You can retain people for service or a job, or you can release people into their destiny. I have been around prominent youth pastors from major global ministries. Their experience and mine as a youth pastor were totally different. Dr. Munroe encouraged me to author books, to become a consultant, to travel, and to become a global leader. He did not insist on me being employed only. He sought to help me find my purpose and destiny and pursue it. That destiny could have been with Bahamas Faith Ministries or outside of Bahamas Faith Ministries. I knew we were joined together for life; so, no matter where I went or what I did, I knew we would always be connected. Help possible successors develop their gifts and allow them to pursue their potential while still being connected.

Principle 9 - MENTOR AND GUIDE IN STAGES

One of my favorite movies of all time is the original *Karate Kid*. In the movie, Mr. Myagi teaches karate to the young Daniel, who is being bullied at school. He assigns Daniel a series of menial, mundane tasks—shining a car ("wax on wax off"), painting a fence—that did not seem to have anything to do with the competition. But later, when he enters the match, young Daniel realizes what Mr. Miyagi was trying to teach him. He prepared Daniel in stages and without revealing the endgame too soon. The tasks seemed boring and meaningless, but Mr. Miyagi used them to communicate a higher purpose.

The individual who has a sense of self-importance may find it insulting to carry their mentor's bags. But this simple task puts them in a position to have access that many will not have and to receive downloads that will become beneficial in the future. A true mentee trusts the mentor and submits to their authority knowing that they are being mentored.

I learned so many things just by being with Dr. Munroe, things which I was able to incorporate into my life. He often encouraged me when he saw that I had grasped a concept or behavior modification that he was trying to communicate without coming out and saying it. His last words to me were that he was proud of me and considered me a trophy of his legacy.

In October 2014, I was speaking for the first time at a New Jersey conference where Dr. Munroe had been the speaker for several years. This was a business conference and one of my strengths was business. The organizer of the conference said when she asked Dr. Munroe about inviting me, she showed him a flier with my photo on it and he pointed at the image and said, "If you have Dave, it's just like having me." Others had told me that Dr. Munroe had said similar things about me, and it was heartwarming to me each time. Many times I followed Dr. Munroe to a city without him making me aware that he had been there, and the people would say to me, "Dr. Munroe spoke about you so highly." Train even when it is not obvious to the trainee or mentee.

Principle 10 - PROVIDE OPPORTUNITIES FOR YOUR POSSIBLE SUCCESSORS TO SIT IN YOUR SEAT OR FUNCTION IN YOUR ARENA

Provide *opportunities* for successors to sit in your seat or seats of power. Create avenues for them to release their gifts. Allow them to shine in their field. If you want people to stick around, you have to provide opportunities for them to excel in their gift. The easiest way to lose good people is to box them in and limit their opportunity to develop. One of the most frustrating situations is for someone who has tremendous potential to be pigeonholed and kept under wraps because a leader fears they may shine if given the opportunity. Some leaders do not want others to shine because they may take away some of their glory. A great leader would never feel this way. Giving a mentee a measured opportunity does not take away from a leader's validity. Good mentors prepare mentees for succession by taking them along and involving them in their world in appropriate settings.

I was given some of the best opportunities possible. I was truly surprised at some of the opportunities Dr. Munroe gave me because I knew such opportunities were not normal and Dr. Munroe had to take liberties with his hosts to include me. I felt special and valued. I recall a few events where this happened. One was at the Shrine Auditorium in Los Angeles, where Dr. Munroe had been invited to a conference by a prominent church. This event involved a number of well known Pastors and Leaders who were either a part of organizing the event or were in attendance. That night there was a long program and many artists and speakers were involved. Praise and worship had gone on for a long time and it was getting late, so I did not expect to be on the platform that night. In fact, I was at the back of the room, near the book table, when Dr. Munroe sent a member of the security team to ask me to come backstage. He said, "I want you to share before I speak." I shared my testimony and afterwards he spoke. It was not something I asked for or pushed my way into. He wanted to expose my gift to the world.

Another event happened in New Orleans. I was at the back of the room and Dr. Munroe called for me. This time, as I began to go backstage, a member of the security team turned me back and would not believe me when I said that Dr. Munroe had called for me. Dr. Munroe corrected the situation and had the same person who had denied me access to him escort me to him. Helen Baylor was the guest artist that night and after she sang I had the opportunity once again to share.

When I was writing my first book, Dr. Munroe set up a meeting with his publisher and asked them to publish my book. They obviously did not want to because I did not have a big ministry and a global television presence. Nonetheless they did it because he insisted. His attitude was to give Dave an opportunity. I ended up authoring several books through his publishers and he and I eventually wrote three books together. In the case of one of them, he simply said, "Add my name to the book you are writing; it will increase your sales." So said so done. I have the unusual distinction of being the only person with whom Dr. Munroe authored a book. The last book we coauthored was *Kingdom Parenting*. I am now completing my twenty-second book, and it all began because he saw fit to put me in position to share my knowledge and gift. You do not have to be the only hero in the movie; give others the opportunity to shine.

Principle 11 - MONITOR AND EVALUATE SUCCESSORS

Evaluate your key people with a view to *strategic placement* based upon identified strengths. Monitoring and evaluation follow a process:

> **T**rain: Impart knowledge and wisdom.
> **T**est: Put possible successor in a position to test their suitability.
> **T**ry: Do not wait for perfection to deploy.

Deploy: Deploy rather than employ. Position "troops" in readiness for assignment.

Evaluate: Assess their performance and suitability.

Release: Release into destiny versus retaining for service.

Principle 12 - THE BEST SUCCESSOR IS THE ONE WHO DOES NOT NEED YOU

Develop people who do not need you. The best person to succeed you is the one who does not need you. The one who is dependent on you will keep looking for you after you are gone. Create partnerships not dependencies. The individual who is not dependent upon you but has been mentored by you can carry on when you are gone. They can lead because knowledge has been transferred to them and they have been prepared to lead. To attempt to lead while looking in the rearview mirror is a recipe for disaster.

Produce people who understand the responsibility that comes with independence and freedom. Freedom is the liberty to fulfill your assignment and pursue your purpose and destiny. Freedom is not the absence of restraint or rules. You can be delivered but not free. Freedom is not a physical state. Nelson Mandela's release date was February 11 1990, but that was not his freedom date. Freedom occurred while he was in prison. As I visited the Apartheid Museum in South Africa, I saw the words he penned describing how he arrived at the point where he became friends with the white guards in prison. He realized they were victims the same as he was. They ended up coming to him for advice and counsel. He also indicated that not forgiving your enemies is like drinking poison and hoping your enemy dies.

Mandela was free long before he left prison. His liberty allowed him to bring together a country that was justifiably full of hate and on the verge of exacting revenge. The demands of freedom are higher **than that of slavery: freedom requires more responsibility**. When you are free you cannot reach back for the comfort of others making decisions for you. Freedom is not working for; freedom is working with. Freedom means responsibility. Dr. Munroe defined freedom as "self-determination under a set of rules that ensure stability… The power to choose between alternatives."

Principle 13 - HANDLE THE EXCHANGE EFFECTIVELY

Never hand off to someone who is not already running. A successor who has never been in the race is not prepared to handle the exchange. You want someone who is already running. You also need someone who is either already running at the same pace or capable of running at the same pace or faster. It is hard to exchange when the next runner cannot keep up. I used to run track, and I remember many baton exchanges. If the outgoing runner did not take off at the right speed, the incoming runner would end up running past him and the exchange would be messed up. You never want to pass the baton to a runner who is slower than you and cannot keep pace for the next leg.

A relay team usually has at least one or two backups. Prepare more than one individual for succession. Make sure you have more than one person capable of succeeding. You may have a primary person identified, but as relay runners know, you need a backup in the event the intended runner is not able to run. Do not throw the baton at your successor and do not drop it to the ground; it must be passed intentionally and at close range. The exchange is normally rehearsed; so, if you know the day is coming, it is time to begin rehearsing the exchange. Remember, you cannot kill a vision, but you can let it die. You cannot kill an idea, but you can ignore it and it will die.

Principle 14 - THE ESSENTIAL INGREDIENT

Succession requires that the mentor and the successor have *courage*. There is no one to "fall back on" or lean on. You must take ownership and responsibility. Remember but do not reminisce. I do not lead by trying to reproduce the way "it used to be." This new focus is why I coined the phrase and spoke it over and repeatedly: "We remember, we honor, we continue." We remember the past, but we cannot live in the past.

It requires *tremendous courage* to follow a legend. Imagine what Joshua faced. Moses was the deliverer, the original hero. The people were already used to Moses and trusted him. Joshua needed courage to follow in the footsteps of Moses, and God knew this. He explained to Joshua the value of courage.

> "Moses My servant is dead. Now therefore, arise, go over
> this Jordan, you and all this people, to the land which I
> am giving to them—the children of Israel. Every place
> that the sole of your foot will tread upon I have given

you, as I said to Moses. From the wilderness and this Lebanon as far as the great river, the River Euphrates, all the land of the Hittites, and to the Great Sea toward the going down of the sun, shall be your territory. No man shall be able to stand before you all the days of your life; as I was with Moses, so I will be with you. I will not leave you nor forsake you. **Be strong and of good courage**, for to this people you shall divide as an inheritance the land which I swore to their fathers to give them. **Only be strong and very courageous**, that you may observe to do according to all the law which Moses My servant commanded you; do not turn from it to the right hand or to the left, that you may prosper wherever you go. This Book of the Law shall not depart from your mouth, but you shall meditate in it day and night, that you may observe to do according to all that is written in it. For then you will make your way prosperous, and then you will have good success. Have I not commanded you? **Be strong and of good courage; do not be afraid, nor be dismayed**, for the LORD your God *is* with you wherever you go." (Joshua 1:2-9. Emphasis added.)

God told Joshua *three times* to be courageous. I understand that admonition.

Myles Munroe with Pastor Dave and BFM Youth.

Myles Munroe and Dave Burrows ministering at Youth Alive.

Ordination of Raymond and Brook Eneas - Nov 2nd.

CHAPTER 7

Running With The Vision

I saw a "quote of caution" on the internet which stated: "We knew the party was over when all we could talk about is our history." Bahamas Faith Ministries celebrates our rich history and legacy because we know we still have a job to do. That job is to run with the vision. We have a lot to talk about beyond our history.

According to the book of Habakkuk, the successor runs with the vision he receives.[6] As successor, the baton was now firmly in my hands, having received it by divine assignment. I fully accepted my assignment. I knew how to run, I knew I could run, I was already running; so, the next step was to rely on my training and preparation to run MY race. Dr. Munroe had done as Apostle Paul said: he had run HIS race; he had

---

6   2.1–3.

finished HIS course. Dr. Munroe was not around to give me advice. Dr. Pinder was not around to give me advice. It was all on me and my leadership team to go out and get the job done. I am so thankful for a great and steady leadership team who partnered with me through the process, especially the initial phases.

That leg of the race began in 2015. We ended 2014 with a series of nine funerals. This was not the way I wanted to start, but it was our reality at the time. That said, 2015 was a year of transition. We still had many crying moments when we remembered certain events. People called us internationally and stated that they had never heard of such a tragedy, where a ministry lost its senior pastor, the church pastor, youth pastor, and the others onboard. Memorial services and other commemorations were being held all over the world—in Africa, Europe, USA, Canada, and even Parliaments of some countries. Each event, although appreciated, reminded us of the loss we experienced and sometimes reopened the wound that was just healing.

Over and over, we relived the events of November 9, 2014. Every BFM service or event—Easter, Mother's Day, Father's Day, Christmas, New Year's—was the first of its kind without Dr. Munroe and Dr. Pinder. Every significant event reminded us that they are no longer here. It was a challenging period. Sometimes their images would appear on the projection screen and everybody would cry. So many moments were awkward. Leading the church, speaking to the staff, communicating with national leaders were all challenging experiences for me standing in the position where Dr. Munroe stood. I was already on the national and international stage but not as his successor.

This was an initial period of refining. Membership support was great. There was tremendous buy-in to the refined vision I presented. Amazingly, while other churches in similar situations were in decline, we were growing. In the early months of 2015, we actually had to place more chairs in the sanctuary. One pastor had told me in November during the days immediately after the crash that people are going to leave the church. You will not know who is really with you, he said, until the new year rolls around. People did not leave en masse; a few left, but more came to fill their places and in 2015 we actually grew by 15 percent.

I knew my job was to streamline and refine. I restructured the board to act like a Cabinet, where each member had a portfolio. I required full PowerPoint presentations by each board member, manager and church council member. I made these changes to delegate authority and ensure that the leadership load was shared. Everyone had to give an account of their stewardship. This requirement stretched some people and caused others to improve their skills. I also knew that one of the reasons Dr. Munroe had wanted me in the first place was because I had an appeal to both generations. We upgraded our technology, added local television programs, increased social media presence, and shortened our service times. We made good changes and difficult changes.

I became very focused, understanding that my only objective was and still is to complete my leg of the race. I also knew that I had to remain humble and remain open. I consulted regularly with my team, and we had many, many meetings. I was team- oriented but decisive. I consulted to gain counsel knowing it was up to me to make decisions. The worst element of leadership is indecision. Indecision in a time of crisis, succession and transition can kill an organization. Right or wrong, decisions must be made, and if you are the leader, it's on you. It is better to correct a wrong decision than to make no decision.

I had to make personal adjustments. My two companies were being run by my wife and I realized the burden on her was becoming great. In addition to running the businesses, she helped me in ministry because I had no assistant. Pastor Kersch Darville, who was slated to become fellowship pastor, was still employed with an offshore bank and was preparing to leave within the next year; but in the meantime, the church had to function and tasks had to be managed. The workload was almost unbearable. I officiated at weddings and funerals. I prepared sermons and preached sermons. I visited people in hospital. I attended national events. I did radio and television interviews. I hosted television programs. I managed finances. I oversaw facility issues, and the list goes on.

My wife and I decided to lease out one of our businesses to focus on the church. This freed up my wife to help me. The irony of this decision was that when Dr. Munroe first approached me about pastoring and I had said no, he said, in the meeting in his living room, with all the board members present, "Don't worry, your wife will help you." He saw something in her that I knew but had never voiced. My wife was always a better pastor than I was. She always knew exactly what to do; she was the one who would stay behind and speak with members after service, like Dr. Munroe did. She was my rock during this time.

The one problem that my wife and I had during this transition period was that things did not go according to plans and we almost lost our business. Revenue declined by 90 percent because the new operator that we leased it to was not ready for what was required to run a successful business. He had never run a retail operation. Our businesses had grown consistently for many years, so we did not expect nor were we prepared for the downturn in revenue. The former employee had been a technician, but I do not believe he ever ran his own business. After seeing a steep decline and the business not performing the way it should we decided to terminate the lease and resume oversight. Ultimately, we saved the business. By the grace of God we not only made it, we excelled in 2015. It was a good year but a rough year.

If 2015 was a year of transition, 2016 was a year of adjustments. I presented to the church the theme for the new year: "Kingdom Reconciliation and Representation. The Year of Recovery – Restoration." We made it successfully through 2015 and it was time to recover and begin to take back lost ground. It was time to represent. I reminded the church that we at Bahamas Faith Ministries needed to represent the Kingdom of God. The Bible speaks of God turning things the enemy meant for evil to our good[7] and I was ready for recovery and restoration. What had been taken away from us needed to be restored. Our souls needed the restoration that the book of Psalms promised.[8]

---

7   For example, Genesis 50.20; John 10.10; Romans 8.28.
8   Psalm 23.3.

We began to introduce new and diverse elements into the ministry. Key among them was KBEN, the Kingdom Business and Empowerment Network. This idea brought all the business people in the ministry into a network to enhance their businesses through networking, training and patronage. Being a business person, I understood the importance and value of successful businesses in furthering the work of the ministry. Too often, business people within the church do not know what each other is doing and do not network. Members are unaware of businesses within the church and, therefore, do not patronize them. When businesses in the church prosper, the church prospers. So, we established the network to bring together the business community in the church and to create awareness of the importance of ownership and economic circulation within the community.

We officially launched what Dr. Munroe had been planning for years, the International Association of Kingdom Churches and Ministries (IAKCM) and held our first Kingdom Believers Summit following on the protocol of the Kingdom Summit that Dr. Munroe had begun. Dr. Munroe had always desired to establish a network specifically to cover churches and ministries, as opposed to the International Third World Leadership Association which focused on leaders from various background like politics, business, professional and social. ITWLA did not have a provision for ecclesiastical covering and administration. Dr. Peter Morgan was the individual Dr. Munroe had called upon to draft the framework for IAKCM, so I leaned on him to make it happen. We held a very successful inaugural conference and began to build on the vision of our visionary leader.

We also introduced several ministries to cater to specific needs of the church, namely, the Keenagers ministry for people older than sixty-five and the Mothers in Zion ministry for women and "mothers" in the church. My wife Angie was the driving force for both. We also began the process of transitioning younger leaders. This was not an easy task as many people who were entrenched in their positions for years found it difficult to move on. I tried to assure them that we were not "getting rid" of anyone, we were simply repositioning them, which, in some cases, may mean moving from player to coach, from follower to leader, or from leader to change agent.

We established a new ministry for millennials called Change Agents to engage millennials and provide a forum for them to contribute to the church and to have upward mobility into leadership. Tremendous shifts have occurred in the world and a major one has been the emergence of millennials. This shift has been a problem for many churches where their millennials either were not engaged or had left the church. When I held my first meeting with our millennials, I asked why most were not involved. I got an interesting answer: they said no one asked and no one had involved them. We had a great exchange and the Change Agents ministry was off and running. Their involvement and ideas proved crucial. We slowly added members of this team to leadership positions thus expanding the leadership base and increasing our reach. We also hired a new youth pastor after not having a youth pastor the first year of transition. The youth ministry had been run by a committee of youth leaders, but we did not have a full-time youth pastor.

In 2016 I launched my weekly column, "Diplomatic Notes," in one of the major local papers. The column featured poignant insight and commentary on national issues from a Kingdom perspective. It was very well received and proved to be a must-read among the local population from all walks of life. Politicians, pastors, community leaders and everyday individuals often referred to the articles and indicated that they were challenged and inspired by them. The Bahamas Government sought our advice on many national issues, which was the norm under Dr. Munroe. The Prime Minister at the time shared that he observed we have a very strong team and he valued our input. We did not agree on all issues, but we stayed engaged.

In 2017 we chose the theme "Activating Kingdom Transformation." Going into our third year we were now positioned to activate some things. We transitioned, we recovered, now it was time to activate. By our third year the ministry was still very strong and stable. Our numbers declined a bit from the previous year but held steady with no significant overall decline. The core membership remained strong and committed and we had new members come in as others left. We added KFIT, our fitness and wellness ministry. I had asked about areas of activation that could benefit the church and we realized that health was a significant and popular issue that needed our attention and could yield significant benefits; therefore we pursued this objective. This ministry focused on healthy eating and exercise and on bringing people together to learn more about health and wellness.

Three years in, we had developed a comfort level. We made sure in 2015 and 2016 to find appropriate ways of honoring our founders. The street leading to the church was renamed Richard Pinder Drive and, as I stated earlier, we tried unsuccessfully to have the main road, Carmichael Road, renamed in Dr. Munroe's honor. We opted in the meantime to rename the Diplomat Center the Myles E. Munroe Diplomat Center.

Myles Munroe Diplomat Center 2023.

The 2018 theme was "Living the Kingdom Mandate." We added Royal Bahamas Defence Force Captain Glen McPhee to the board and adopted the perpetual theme of "Upgrade, Expand and Build," signaling that we expected not merely to maintain our present status but to move forward exponentially. Our transition to younger leadership accelerated as we moved the younger generation to leadership in the Kingdom Business and Empowerment Network.

That year, 2018, also saw the launch of the Second Chance program initiated by Orlando "Landlord" Miller, who had come to the ministry as a gang member. He was now a husband, father, businessman, international recording artist, and mentor. He was grateful for the transformation that had been accomplished in his life and wondered how he could give back. We collaborated and came up with the second chance program, which involved bussing fifty to a hundred and fifty youth from the inner city or as referred to in Nassau, the over-the-hill and heritage communities to the Diplomat Center every Friday for instruction, mentorship and fun. We also fed the young people, which for some meant their only meal of the day. The ministry overall remained on a very firm foundation and we continued to progress in building the vision. All ministries and systems were functioning and we were running with the vision.

Our 2019 theme was "Restoring Kingdom Dominion, Culture and Community." During this year, our transition to younger leadership accelerated and impacted the children's church ministry and other ministries. Transitions were not easy because our leaders in these areas had served faithfully for many years. But I knew we needed younger leadership to perpetuate the vision. Despite the challenges, we transitioned successfully. We made sure that as we welcomed the new leaders, we honored the leaders who had transitioned.

With new leadership we saw an expansion of the involvement of children in our services, particularly on Children's Day, which featured child speakers for the Sunday morning main service. In fact, in both the children's and youth services, the children and youth conducted the entire service, including dance, singing and even teaching and preaching. I made a very important decision during this period, that at any service where the entire church was together, we would have both children and youth involved in the services and visible on the platform.

If children and youth are allowed only to sit in a service and spectate, an invisible divide is created that makes them feel held hostage by adults for a meeting that is not theirs; in other words, it's an adult service and they are there by default and not by choice. We ensured that our children and youth had active roles in the life of the church. This decision had a dual positive effect. It significantly improved and raised the morale of the children and youth and it spurred the attendance of their parents, who came out to see their children involved in the service.

We incorporated new elements in the Sunday service that on occasion included live drama or video segments often produced by young people. Unfortunately, in September of 2019 we were thrust into the national limelight as hurricane Dorian hit The Bahamas, particularly Abaco and Grand Bahama. BFM led the way in the midst of this challenge. We successfully partnered with the government to feed thousands, providing food essentials, generators and building materials to help people recover and rebuild. Our Freeport campus, which had been established years earlier under Dr. Munroe, played a critical role in this process. We rented a

5,000 square feet warehouse in Freeport and another 3,000 square feet in Nassau and had containers brought in through many international partners. We sent teams from our Nassau campus weekly to serve and assist.

Major ministries in the United States sent both teams and donations to assist in rebuilding. The government commended us for our leadership, and agencies such as the Red Cross partnered with us because we showed we have efficient systems in place that enhance distribution efforts. In 2019 we also officially established our third campus. Pastor Raymond Eneas, a son of the ministry, was pastoring in Orlando and we decided to incorporate the Orlando church as our first US-based church campus. Pastor Eneas also assumed leadership of the Freeport campus, an unusual step but one that was necessary and helped to stabilize our campus structure.

Our 2020 theme was "Manifesting Kingdom Lifestyle and Culture." We did not know that we and the country were about to experience a double whammy. On the heels of the ravages of hurricane Dorian was the COVID-19 pandemic. We faced this great challenge with the rest of the world. The pandemic created an unprecedented period of uncertainty and logistical nightmares.

We know that challenges are also opportunities; so, we confronted the challenge head-on and made necessary adjustments and improvisations not only to survive but to thrive. For the first time, the church-world was forced to conduct services and maintain the body of believers through streaming. In-person services were not allowed. People were dying from the virus in unprecedented numbers and the world was in both turmoil and panic.

Very early in the pandemic, we assessed that our leadership would have to be innovative and courageous; so we met as a team and mapped out strategies for the way ahead. We formed a COVID-19 task force consisting of doctors, nurses, nutritional experts, pharmacists, and strategic individuals to develop a comprehensive plan on how to manage the crisis. One of our first actions was to orchestrate the shift from in-person to online services. This meant ensuring that our technology was ahead of the curve. We already had a very significant online footprint through our own streaming service along with Facebook and YouTube, this technology was no longer an accessory to ministry, it was the primary element of ministry.

We quickly upgraded our technology and moved to add Zoom as a feature in our service options. Fortunately, we were pre-positioned to lead in this area and saw great success on both the local and international levels. Interestingly, our international following grew as people from all over the world who were not able to attend church began to tune in to our services every Sunday. We showed them on our screens and some of these followers challenged us in ways we had not thought about before. Our online congregation began to ask to become actual members of our church. They insisted on going through the membership class and becoming full-fledged members even though many had never been to an in-person service in The Bahamas. Not having our congregation in person on Sundays was a great challenge, but we adjusted and thrived.

In August 2020 I received a call to serve as chaplain of the Bahamas Parliament (House of Assembly). This meant that every week, before

Parliament began its deliberations, I had the opportunity to share a devotional message and lead the legislature in prayer. The Prime Minister, Cabinet ministers, backbenchers, and other members of Parliament all voiced their appreciation for the inspiration provided through my devotions. At times I wondered what impact, if any, I was having, but when members would come to me and ask for my notes and even the scriptures I used, I realized I was making a difference. Interestingly, when the government changed in late 2021, the incoming Prime Minister Phillip Davis singled me out at a business event and thanked me for those inspirational messages. He noted that they encouraged him while he was leader of the Opposition in Parliament.

In spite of the initial financial challenges of 2020, we were able to weather the storm and actually see God's provisions increase, allowing us not merely to maintain but to build and grow. As 2020 came to a close, a critical event happened that would have a major impact on our ministry. A young man, Andrew "Drew" Gardiner, who had grown up in the ministry, approached me through his father about ways we could improve our services. He was both a professional singer and artist and a media expert. He had been off to college and had now returned home. He presented ideas to us both visually and verbally that would alter the course of our church. He showed clear paths to enhanced efficiency in our worship experience and in our online footprint.

We met with over one hundred and fifty of our crucial leaders and began to map the way forward to an upgraded version of BFM. This meant incorporating younger people into our worship team, our media department and other critical areas. We needed someone to drive the process and so we hired Mr. Gardiner.

As 2021 rolled in, the upgrade continued under the new theme of "Kingdom Restoration and Recovery." We now had a well-established and well-oiled ministry. Our upgraded media and worship experience positioned us for our members' return to in-person services. In the beginning, the numbers were low because the pandemic had not subsided and there were lulls and spikes causing fear and trepidation about coming to the church building.

Despite the slow start, we continued to progress. The church's recovery from the restrictions of the pandemic was now fully underway and we were gearing up for a big comeback. Like many churches around the world, attendance continued to fluctuate. COVID outbreaks were still occurring, which caused people who would attend church under normal circumstances to hesitate, particularly the elderly, who were advised by doctors to avoid public spaces because of their vulnerabilities. Nevertheless, we were well positioned and, in fact, upgraded and enhanced as we prepared for the future. This future began in 2021 with a surge in people from around the world coming to Bahamas Faith Ministries to be baptized. They had amazing testimonies of being blessed during the pandemic by our online presence. Our cyber members hailed from such places as India, Pakistan, Dubai, Egypt, Cameroon, Nigeria, Ireland, New Zealand, and Australia.

Cyber member visiting Diplomat Center and Baptism.

Amazingly, too, before the end of 2021, we paid off our mortgage debt and acquired crucial equipment through the giving of our local and international members and the generosity of the Munroe Global Foundation led by Myles Munroe Jr. and Charisa Munroe and the Zamar

Group led by Andrew Gardiner Sr. We emerged from the pandemic years strong and well positioned for the future.

Myles Munroe Jr. and Charissa Munroe with Governor General at BFM renaming

In 2022 our theme was "Kingdom Empowerment." We wanted to empower our members for great exploits. This empowerment included spiritual empowerment, intellectual empowerment, business empowerment, and leadership empowerment. We embarked on new training programs through special training events and our weekly online Kingdom School of Empowered Living.

That year also meant additional transitions, particularly with our Worship and Fine Arts ministry. In evaluating that ministry, I realized that some of our leaders were now in or approaching their sixties. We needed to engage younger leaders in order to be properly prepared and positioned for the future. This again was a challenging period because faithful leaders were being asked to take a step back to make room for younger leaders. Our longtime worship leader Minister Tracy Knowles transitioned out as leader of the Worship and Fine Arts ministry and allowed Vincent "Vmac" McDonald to assume the leadership role.

Some of the older leaders also moved on and some remained as we welcomed a cadre of new younger worship leaders. This was an exciting time as we experienced the innovative ideas of youth combined with the wisdom of the older generation. We successfully managed this transition and emerged with a new energized Worship and Fine Arts and Media ministry that brought new life to the church.

In 2023 our theme was "Kingdom Transformation." The motto and defining statement of purpose of BFM has always been transformational: "We transform followers into leaders and leaders into agents of change." This is who we are and always have been. This transformation, we know, can happen only through the Kingdom being made manifest on earth. As a ministry we have always had and continue to have strategic national and global impact. Our members are positioned for high-level influence "into all the world," as Jesus said. We have produced leaders in government, business, ministry, social services, medicine, military, and many other spheres of influence. Our members have sat in Parliament and on strategic boards, headed global corporate entities, launched powerful and profitable business entities.

We have always known our purpose and mission, and as we continued our mission in 2023, we focused once again on training and developing leaders to change their environments. Thankfully, we began to see our in-person numbers climb, on occasion approaching pre-pandemic numbers. We observed that there had been a paradigm shift in the way "people do church"— they were splitting their attendance between in-person and online attendance. This is a new reality that we are focused on adjusting to, and we are strategically positioning ourselves to be ahead of the curve.

At the time of writing, we are in the year 2024. Early this year I became a consultant to another government when the Government of the Turks and Caicos Islands contracted me to advise on and implement a program to reach young people, especially those involved in gangs and criminal activity. This engagement was another expansion of the vision of BFMI and a follow through of what Dr. Myles Munroe had begun globally. Our global reach and outreach continue. We and members of our church have ministered in Israel, South Africa, Australia, New Zealand, Zambia, Eswatini (Swaziland), Ireland, Scotland, Canada, Netherlands, United Kingdom, The Philippines, Germany, Colombia, Brazil, and many more.

This year will mark ten years since the departure of our founders. We have decided to commemorate our legacy and this anniversary with a special series of events. This book is one of the elements of our legacy year. November will mark a period of remembrance, commemoration and recognition as we prepare for greater future impact.

We were established as a local church with a global vision and have now transitioned to a global church with a global vision and footprint.

Training Youth Leaders In Canada

Recent Baptism of members at the beach.

Defense force cadets visit BFM.

Cyber members becoming official memberss of BFM via Zoom.

Pastor Dave with the speaker of the house serving as Parliamentary Chaplain.

Pastor Dave with inner-city young men.

Pastor Dave and Angie with Charlie Masala
visiting the hospital where Nelson Mandela was staying 2013.

Pastor Dave and Angie and Myles and Ruth with Hon. Daniel Johnson - Minister of Youth.

Munroe's and Burrows with Robyn and Marilyn Gool
(Pastor Dave's sister), Dr Johnson and Ghandi Pinder.

p 118 - Pastor Dave and team at the Governor General's residence for the official presentation.

Pastor Dave with children at BFM Nursery.

Pastor Dave with inmates at Bahamas Fox Hill prison.

Pastor Dave and Angie and Pastors with
Defence Force Commander Tellis Bethel and Terri Bethel and Cadets.

Pastor Dave and team with Governor General.

BFM Team providing food during Covid Pandemic.

Young man from Netherlands who was impacted by messages of Dr. Munroe.

Wife of President, Vice President and wife of Eswatini (Swaziland).

Young man from South Africa who was impacted by Dr. Munroe and BFM.

Delegation from Eswatini visiting the Myles Munroe Diplomat Center.

Pastor Kersch Darville with global cyber member being baptized in Nassau, Bahamas.

Former Vice President of Nigeria visiting Pastor Dave at BFM

Young people responding to altar all at special event.

Teenage youth leaders ministering to their peers with Youth Pastor Corey Rolle.

Pastor Dave speaking to thousands of leaders at Empowered 21 Africa event.

BFM Sunday Service crowd post pandemic.

BFM 2023-2024.

BFM 2023-2024.

BFM 2023-2024.

THE YOUTH AND FAMILY CENTER

Emerge Youth Center_ Nassau, Bahamas   07.20.2018   TDG ARCHITECTS

Emerge Youth Center_ Nassau, Bahamas   07.20.2018   TDG ARCHITECTS

Emerge Youth Center_ Nassau, Bahamas   07.20.2018

Emerge Youth Center_ Nassau, Bahamas   07.20.2018

Emerge Youth Center_ Nassau, Bahamas 07.20.2018 TDG ARCHITECTS

BASKETBALL/VOLLEYBALL COURT

Emerge Youth Center_ Nassau, Bahamas 07.20.2018 TDG ARCHITECTS

www.ingramcontent.com/pod-product-compliance
Lightning Source LLC
Chambersburg PA
CBHW050443150626
46551CB00028B/1169